You've Got It All Wrong
A Teen Story Collection from
WE ARE ABSOLUTELY NOT OKAY.Org

Destiny Allison
Summer Cooper
Isabel Cordova
Kristina Edgar
Ethan Elliott
Tattiyanna Fernandez
Corinna J. Flaherty
LaDawn Harris
Brayan Hernandez
Delanie Higbee
Maggie Higgins
Nina Hogan
Jacquie Lampignano
Christopher Milbrad
Kelly Peterson
Caleb "Joey" Reed
Lupita Ruelas
Natanael Santamaria
Angel Seumptewa
Elizabeth Tapia
Deanna Tittle

Edited by Marjie Bowker and Ingrid Ricks
For privacy reasons, some names have been changed

You've Got It All Wrong

Copyright © 2014
by Edmonds School District

ISBN: 978-0-9894381-0-0

All RIGHTS RESERVED

Cover Design by: Jacquie Lampignano

Edited and compiled by Marjie Bowker and Ingrid Ricks

Proofreading by Risa Laib

Print book and ebook formatting by Hydra House
www.hydrahousebooks.com

Published by Scriber Lake High School

www.weareabsolutelynotokay.org

TABLE OF CONTENTS

OUR INTENTION WITH
THIS STORY COLLECTION

"Freak," "Druggie," "Slut," "Loser." All of us have felt the sting of labels, and the things people say can stick like nametags. But are they true? Do these labels define us?

Imagine how perceptions might change if—instead of instantly labeling someone—we all took a close second look and got to know one another and the challenges we've faced?

At Scriber Lake High School, we are all about taking that second look. Here we recognize that everyone has a story, and that knowing each other's stories is the key to true understanding and community. Facing reality isn't easy. Some of us have struggled with the ramifications of being completely honest and transparent. But we believe we are taking hold of our futures in a positive, powerful way by revisiting our pasts through our narratives. Our experiences have labeled us "troubled teens," but we choose to label ourselves "mature teens who have learned from our pasts."

Only you know the full truth about events in your past—about the hard situations you've found yourself in and the decisions you chose to make. And only you know exactly what emotions were associated with all of it. We hope that our stories will encourage you to grow from your experiences, and help you know that there are people out there who want to listen to you with respect.

ONE SHOT

BRAYAN HERNANDEZ

I was nervous. I could feel my heart beating as if I had just run for miles. My whole body was tense and as the seconds went by, I started to tremble.

"Where is he?" I asked, forcing my voice to sound tough and in control.

"Basketball Court," my homeboy said.

I started walking down one of the halls at my middle school, making my way to the indoor court. *It's time, I'm ready,* I told myself repeatedly, trying to pump myself up. A feeling of paranoia swept through my body. My hands, which I'd clenched into fists, started twitching. I didn't know how I was going to confront this guy. Different lines went through my head as I tried hard to think which one would be best.

I caught him playing basketball at the far corner of the gym. He didn't have a clue I was coming, and he didn't know what I was up to. I walked up to him, got in his face and showed him my blue flag. I wasn't part of a gang yet, but I was representing the colors of the gang I wanted to join. He was a member of the Bloods and their main color was red. During school lunch the day before, a friend who had a brother in the gang I worshiped told me that the new kid was a Blood and that he was going to grab the flag that hung from my pocket and step on it in front of me. The Blood never came to my face and told me, so I had to take care of the matter myself. This would be my chance to prove myself to the gang.

"Heard you tell someone you was going to grab my flag and step on it in front of my face!" I screamed at the boy. My heart palpitated and I could feel every ounce of blood rushing through my system.

"I never said nothing, dawg," he replied. He was eleven or twelve and stood about five foot three, a couple of inches taller than I was. He had long black hair tied up in a ponytail. He wore a red 49ers hat and looked Asian American.

I was starting to sense that my friend had made up the whole story about him wanting to grab my flag and stomp on it. But I didn't care. This was my chance to show what I could do.

"Fuck your hood, homie!" I screamed.

❧

Ever since my cousin had joined the gang a few months back, I had been tagging along with him and hanging out at what was called a "safe house." At first it was used as a place to smoke pot. The gang didn't have a problem with me being there; they thought it was fun to have a little homie running around the house. They treated me like a kid brother. All this time I sat back minding my own business and watching what they would do. I was very curious and couldn't help eavesdropping every once in a while. I heard them talk about different gang problems and observed two or three drugs deals every time I was there. I figured they weren't interested in having a youngster in the hood because they didn't have the time to be taking care of a kid. I started noticing all the drug deals, the money and the parties. It was like nothing I had ever seen. It grabbed my attention and soon I couldn't think about anything else but being like them.

About two weeks before my run-in with the Blood, I was rolling along with my cousin. It was a sunny day, the sound system was loud and we had the windows down. The thought had been going through my head for a while and I couldn't keep it in any longer.

"I want to be in the gang," I blurted. I couldn't believe the words came out of my mouth. For a second, I wished I could have taken them back, but I couldn't hold them in anymore. My hope was for him to take it smooth and say yes. But if he didn't, I knew it was going to be bad.

"What the fuck? Are you stupid?" My cousin, who was four years older than me, looked at me like I was insane.

"Yeah, fool, I want to be like you," I replied.

My cousin was always a funny guy but when I said that his face went completely dark. I could see the vein on his right temple pulsating. He turned to look at me, his eyes glowing with fury. I couldn't stand his glare and turned away as quickly as I could.

"You are too young for shit like this," he finally exclaimed.

I was expecting that answer, but I wasn't going to let him put me off like that.

"I know I'm young, but I just want to be part of the crew. Help me out, Carnal."

I tried not to make it sound like I was begging him. I could feel the tension between us. He hardened his grip on the wheel and started shifting the clutch brusquely. His face was red and hard.

"Naw. I don't want to be responsible for anything stupid you do. Your parents are already blaming me for your bad grades and for always having you out. I don't want any more shit from them, alright!?"

I didn't have a comeback for that and I could tell he wanted the conversation to be over. He stepped on the pedal like he was trying to get away from someone.

I didn't say anything after that and he didn't either. There was a moment of silence and then he turned the music up again.

After that ride with my cousin, it seemed like he was trying to avoid me. He usually picked me up every day and didn't drop me off till late at night. But throughout the next week, he only scooped me up twice and only for a few hours. When I was with him, he did invite me to smoke a joint, but there was a sense of discomfort floating in the smoke that we were inhaling.

Discouraged and disappointed that my cousin wasn't willing to help me, I decided to handle it on my own.

A week after our confrontation, my cousin was at work and I didn't have anything to do so I walked to the safe house just to kick it and smoke. The shot caller was there. He was the one who told the gang what to do, what was right and what wasn't. He was about five foot nine, skinny and bald from shaving his head. He was eighteen. He wore a pair of black chucks, khaki Dickies-style pants and a white t-shirt, both nicely ironed with a crease. When he saw me smoking a bowl, he walked over and sat beside me.

"You want some?" I asked.

"Naw, I'm cool," he replied.

I exhaled the smoke and took a deep breath. I didn't know what to say, but I knew this was my opportunity.

"I want to be part of the gang, Gee."

He looked startled, then mugged at me straight in my eyes and laughed.

"Ha-ha what? How old are you lil homie?" he asked.

"I'm twelve," I said proudly.

I watched him grab his chin and shake his head, still smiling.

"This ain't no fun and games, lil one," he replied.

"I know," I returned.

He looked over at me again. I just stared at him, trying to penetrate his gaze. This had to go well. This was my only chance left. If he said "no," then that was it for me. I didn't want this conversation to turn out the same way it did with my cousin, but I didn't want my cousin to feel disrespected because I didn't listen to him, either. I wanted this, though, and I was going to do whatever it took to be like him.

"You want to be in the hood? You gotta keep it real," he said finally.

"I'm trying to keep it real," I replied, my eyes still locked on his. "That's why I'm asking."

It was a crucial moment, but I felt hopeful. I knew that stepping up like this had to have an impact on him. Usually gang members had to recruit people for them to be allowed into the gang. But I had taken matters into my own hands. At only twelve years old, I was stepping up on my own.

He shook his head again, but I could tell that he was thinking about my request.

"You want to do that shit? Then fuck it. But you gotta prove yourself because I ain't about to have a lil youngster running around claiming something and when the time comes, you be running scared." The look on his face had changed. He was no longer smiling. He was serious. I knew he was telling me that if I was going to be in, I had to man up as quickly as I could.

"Nah, it ain't even like that," I replied.

I felt calm and more assured. The pressure had lifted.

"Alright then. What do you want to be when you grow up then?" he asked.

"I want to be a gangsta like all of you," I said in a loud voice.

He laughed. "How old are you again?" he asked. His gaze rose and he smiled with only the right corner of his mouth.

"I'm twelve," I replied.

"Damn. That makes you the youngest in the hood!" he replied with a laugh.

"Yeah, but that don't matter," I quickly shot back.

"Prove it then."

That was the last thing he said. He got up and headed for the only private room that was available for them. The homeless family who provided the house already took up the rest of the place. I knew that room was used to do harsher drugs like cocaine, to clean and hide guns, or just to relax and hang out if you didn't want to chill in the living room.

I sat there thinking for a minute. Then I took a hit and laughed. All I knew was that from then on, I had to prove it. This talk was the exact thing I needed to go further. But what was I going to do?

❧

The Blood pushed me. Out of nowhere, he squeezed his right palm into a fist, leaned back and got me with a righty across my left cheek, sending me flying backward onto the shiny wooden floor. I was surprised he took the first blow. My head was spinning and throbbing and before I could react, he was on top of me, pounding on my left eyebrow. The more his fists came in contact with my skin, the less pain I felt. It got to the point where my eyebrow went numb. I could feel my face swelling. It was like it had inflated and almost doubled in size. Dozens of students, even the loner kid in the corner of the gym, gathered to watch. I could hear someone saying, "Damn, he getting his ass whooped!" and heard others cheering me on, saying, "Come on, Brayan. Get up!"

The blows to my face were nothing compared to the realization that I was blowing my chance at joining the gang. I couldn't let this fool embarrass me like this. I couldn't go down. I wasn't going to throw this chance away. Plus, everyone was watching. If I let this keep going instead of proving myself, I was going to be the laugh around the school for a long time.

I was determined. Somehow I got the strength and flipped him off me. I grabbed his long hair with my left hand and started hitting him with my right fist around his eyes and nose. I lost control.

This ain't enough. You got to suffer! I was thinking in my mind. The more I hit him, the crueler I wanted to be. Rage took over me. If I could have, I would have tried to kill him or done anything possible so he wouldn't ever get up. I wanted his face to be unrecognizable. His face puffed up like mine. A burst of blood shot out of his nose and splashed all over my fist and onto the gym floor. I felt like a champion, like I had been beaten up and made the greatest comeback in history.

The supervising teacher finally noticed there was a fight and came running over to separate us.

"Stop, stop!!" he yelled as he pulled me off.

I wasn't done.

"Get the fuck off of me!" I screamed. I tried to shake him off but he was gripping me hard around my upper body with his arms.

"You need to calm down," he urged. I felt like a caged animal that had just been robbed of its prey.

The teacher took me out the back door where the security guard was waiting. Before we got there, he asked, "You got anything you don't want them to see?"

I gave him my blue flag.

He shook his head. I knew he had always liked me.

"You realize you in deep trouble, my man?"

"I really don't give a damn, I'm just real happy right now," I answered, laughing.

The security guard took me to the security office. I couldn't think clearly and my heart was still pumping. All I could think about was the guy I'd fought and his bloody, fucked-up face.

Moments later the vice principal walked in. I hated her. She had the skinniest legs with the broadest body in this world and a face that looked like a toad.

"How are you feeling?" she asked in a sarcastic tone.

"Better than ever," I replied with a smirk.

She called my parents. My mom couldn't get out of work but my dad could. When I saw him walk through the office doors, I couldn't even look him in the face. I already knew what was waiting for me. I would either be expelled or suspended for a while because I had been suspended multiple times before this; each time it happened, the length of time increased.

The vice principal called for an interpreter, who explained the situation in Spanish to my dad.

Once he was filled in, she looked at me in disgust. "Your actions have really stunned us," she said. "Do you have anything at all you want to say?"

I said nothing. I just stared at the ground. I was worried about what my dad had to say, but I didn't give two fucks about what this woman had to say.

I left the school with a month-long suspension. My dad didn't speak until we were back in the car.

"You're disappointing us," he said finally. "All we wanted to do was to give you everything we never had, all our sweat and hard-earned money to bring you and your sister here and you are already throwing it away."

As usual, I said nothing when he talked to me. I felt bad, but the excitement of what I had just done faded all those feelings. I was happy, but knew not to show it.

He took me home and went back to work. He had told me on the drive home that I was being punished until my suspension was lifted, but

I took that as "a couple days and you're cool."

I lived about a block away from the high school my cousin attended. I had gotten home just when their lunch started. None of the homies from the gang went to school but they were always there at lunch, hollering at the girls who passed by and smoking pot in the corner. I texted my cousin to tell him what happened. He told me to come out and meet him.

My eyebrow had swelled up pretty good so I grabbed my Locs shades. I felt satisfied and proud as I put them on. I walked the block to the school and met up with him and his homies.

"Why you wearing shades, lil homie?" one of them asked when they saw me.

"Look for yourself," I replied.

When I removed the shades, they all laughed in surprise. I felt a rush of pride surge through me.

"I got in a fight with a slob."

A slob is a derogatory term for the word "blood," which means "slow or retarded." They all gathered around me, smiling and laughing. It was the kind of laugh that makes people feel accepted, like they belonged.

"Damn, homie. That's what's up. You whoop his ass or what?" one of them asked.

"Hell yeah, I did. He got good hits though, I ain't going to lie," I replied.

"That's cool that's cool," they all said, patting me on the head. As usual they were passing a blunt around. A couple of females were around, too, so I took a long hit, trying to look even tougher than I felt.

When lunch was over, we all shook hands and headed our separate ways. I had to get home before my mom showed up.

Today was perfect, I thought as I started walking. I didn't have to look in the mirror to know I had the biggest smile on my face. I had made an impression. They knew I had what it took to be a gangster.

Walking home, I didn't have a clue that soon I would have to commit a robbery at gunpoint in order to prove myself even further. I didn't know that I would have to get jumped on by multiple homies that were already in the gang, or that I would get brutally beaten twice for at least thirteen seconds—once for induction into the South Side like any other Southern gang from California, the other time to get into the actual gang. I didn't know that I would soon be selling drugs, stealing and learning how a drive-by shooting is done. I didn't know that I would watch a homie get shot, and I didn't know that I was going to come face-to-face with death and almost get killed only one hundred feet from my own apartment. Most of all, I didn't know that my cousin would witness a murder and that the gang I so desperately wanted to be a part of would eventually turn on him.

All I knew as I walked home was that I wanted to be a full-fledged gangster representing the best color, the right color, the color blue. And I figured it was only a matter of time before my wish came true.

A Note From Brayan

After three years of living in the chaos of gang life, I got out when my cousin was implicated in the murder mentioned at the end of my story. The gang turned on him, which affected me. He cooperated with police and was given immunity, but he made some bad choices and was deported to Mexico. I was expelled from school for gang affiliation and drug use. I went to rehab as an outpatient and have been clean and sober ever since, but my school didn't let me back in. That's when I came to Scriber. Last year, I told my story for the first time in Scriber's first published book, *We Are Absolutely Not Okay*. I felt like a can of soda being opened to release all of the fizz; all the negative energy that I had built over the years poured out and I lost the chains that were holding me back. Before, I was afraid to tell my story because of what everyone would think of me. But I found that instead of seeing me as a bad person, people saw me as someone who wanted to use his past to help other young people in similar situations. In the last year, I have been asked to share my story in front of many groups, and have been surprised at how much this has helped me to find a voice of hope for others. I have also learned how to become a leader. I plan to study criminal justice at Everett Community College and will start an internship with the Lynnwood Police Department after graduation this spring.

FLY AWAY ANGEL BABY

ANGEL SEUMPTEWA

I hear my sister's phone ring as we walk into Walgreens and my stomach drops. I know it's my mom.

"Angel was told to be home at two o'clock!" she bellows at Krischelle.

I can feel myself go numb. I've spent Easter weekend in Flagstaff with my sister and I am supposed to be heading home to Winslow, a sixty-mile bus ride.

"Why can't Angel stay for a little longer?" Kris asks.

"I don't want her to turn out like you!" Mom yells.

"What the hell is that supposed to mean?" Kris yells back. When she starts to get angry her eyebrow twitches.

"Shut the hell up!" Mom yells.

I feel my anger rise, then it just numbs into nothing again.

"Forget it. I'm keeping her until later," Kris declares defiantly. "When she gets home don't be such a bitch to her!" Without letting my mom finish, Kris hangs up.

Krischelle is living with her last born, Hali, and her fiancé, Marty. When I was six years old, my sister became my guardian due to my mom's prison sentence for her third DUI. Even though Kris and I were thirteen years apart, we were inseparable. Yet we haven't seen each other for four years.

I fear what my mom will say or do if I come home late, so I tell my sister, "I'll just go home. I don't want mom to yell at you anymore."

Kris's face is beet red, but her eyes are puppy-like. "No! I finally got you here to Flagstaff," she whimpers. "Mom can wait for once. Angel, why not just come live with me?"

I don't really like the idea of living with her because she and her fiancé are into doing drugs. I also don't know Marty, so I am very wary of him. I'm used to seeing my parents and siblings smoke marijuana and use other drugs, so I just act like I don't know what they are doing.

"I have grandma to take care of," I say.

Grandma isn't sick. She's fit as a horse. Mom just wanted to become the caregiver of my grandma because she can get money for watching her. My grandma was the one to take care of me when I was a baby, so I think of her as my mother. I want Kris to know how much my grandma means to me.

"You're only fourteen!" she says.

I answer her seriously. "If I don't take care of her, who will? Mom's just a drunk. She rarely ever watches grandma."

Sadly, she says, "Okay, Mano. You have a bigger heart than the rest of us."

Kris says this because even if I get beaten up and talked down, I keep my head up and smile. So I listen to Kris and decide to stay longer. Nervousness is coming, but I shut it out and enjoy the rest of the day.

I take the Greyhound and get in to Winslow at 9 p.m., seven hours later than I was supposed to be home. My brother, Seffen, doesn't come to pick me up like my mom had planned. I rarely go anywhere without my mom. I'm not even allowed to go hang out with friends. I only go from home to school, then back.

I call my mom, with worry, and ask her, "Where's Seffen?"

"Find your own way home," she slurs into the phone.

"Okay," I answer, not caring.

My mom's an alcoholic; it runs in the genes. So she drinks herself into a daze every day. She's had this drinking problem since before I was born; when my siblings told me she was sober during each of our pregnancies, I didn't believe them. I don't know how she was able to be without alcohol for that long. With or without money, she will always find a drink. Sometimes she makes me persuade my grandmother for money, sometimes she goes to her friends. Her friends don't care because she also buys for them when she has money.

I decide to walk the two miles from the bus stop to my house. Just as I step off North Park Drive I hear sirens zip down the street. Thinking the police are going to my house, I start to walk faster. When my brother and mom drink, they end the night by fighting, so I worry about my grandma trying to break up the fight. Usually it's a two-person job that we do together. The neighbors always call the police, so when the police come they know my mom and brother by first names. Then I slow down because I realize I wouldn't hear the sirens if they were going to my house. The police station is just down the street from our apartment, which is still at least a mile away from where I am now.

I walk slowly, taking the back roads. I hear crickets singing their nightly melody and the light posts flicker on and off, in a rhythm, trying to stay on. If the lights go out I know the roads like the back of my palm. I'm not afraid of anything but the consequences I am going to face when I get home. I put the things my mom is most likely to say to me in a list:

1. "Who the hell do you think you are?"
2. "I know I shouldn't have let you go to Flagstaff."
3. "You and your sister are ungrateful little asses."

To take my mind off of this, I start to think about how much fun I had with my sister and niece. Even though my sister was high, she took me to the mall to go shopping. We rode on the public bus, which was always my favorite thing to do when I was younger. My sister doesn't know that I myself started following the rest of my family's drug use. I don't want her to judge me and lose the trust she has for me. If I hadn't been with my brother Seffen, I wouldn't have started smoking and drinking. Seffen is my supplier and the only person in my family who knows I am following down the path that I was always afraid to go down.

Before I know it, I am walking up the stairs to our corner apartment. When I get to the front door, I stop and take three deep breaths to work up all the courage I have before I face my mom.

Just as I open the door, my brother spots me and, staggering, pulls me inside. My courage already disappearing, I start to shake and let him pull me, knowing I can't get out of his grip. Seffen is a nineteen-year-old, 165-pound problem child, but he's the favorite one out of five children. He is the real baby; my mom treats him like he's her only child. I don't understand why Seffen is her favorite even though he was the first one to go to prison out of us kids. At first I was sad that he had to go to prison. But after that, all I said was that it was his fault because he should have known better than to steal from his job.

When Seffen is sober he tries to be brotherly, but once he has his alcohol he shows his true feelings. He always tells me that I am adopted or that I'm a freak, and he always finds things to throw at me. I am afraid to be around him when he is drunk, because he usually chases me around with knives trying to kill me. Seffen is always drunk; it's just gotten worse lately. He drinks like it's a game.

Laughing and slurring, he says, "You're stupid for coming home."

"I know," I agree in a whispered voice. Just like my brother, my mom also shows her true self when she's drunk. She tells me she wishes I was never born, or that I'm not her child.

Seffen is pulling me past the living room where my grandma sits during the day, while my mom drinks in the bedroom.

As he pushes me into the bedroom, I see my mom—with her feet resting on a couple of trash bags full of my packed clothes—guzzle the rest of a half pint of 90 proof peppermint schnapps. She's missing an earring, which I notice is in her bird nest of hair. Makeup smeared, one of her pant legs is up past her knee.

She looks at me with disgust in her eyes. "You ungrateful little bastard!" she slurs. "I knew I shouldn't have let you go to that slut of a sister."

I stop shaking. I'm a little more comfortable, thinking all that is going to come from my mom is verbal abuse.

My mom calls Krischelle a slut because she had her first kid at fifteen. I wince, wanting to say, "Why do you call Kris a slut? Look at how many guys you sleep with." I can count and name all of them. She finds most of them at the bar, and they always come back for more. But I keep my mouth shut. I don't want to get hit again for defending my sister.

Mom keeps muttering things I can't understand. Then, accusingly, she asks, "Who did you sleep with?"

I'm annoyed but I keep it hidden, because I knew this question would come. When I hide my true feelings it's a lot easier to deal with, and I won't get into so much trouble. Every time my mom gets going on my sister being a slut, she turns it on me being a slut.

"No one," I say, looking her straight in the eyes. Wrong move. I've learned that if you look mom in the eyes she will think you are trying to start a fight.

I drop my gaze. "May I go take a shower?"

Asking a question is a lot better, because I know my mom will beat me for being disrespectful if I get up and walk away.

She gets even madder when I look her in the eyes again. She must think I'm testing her. She gets up, grabs a handful of my hair, pulls me to the bathroom and then pushes me inside. I think that this might be the only physical thing coming from her, but I am mistaken.

Just as I am ready to close the door, she comes bounding in. No words from her, just one eyebrow up and a smirk on her face saying, "Ready?" I'm terrified; my heart is pounding. I want to scream but I can't. Soft sobs are all that come out. I know she is ready to start her beating because she cracks her knuckles. I can't defend myself or it will last even longer. She has beaten me up a few times; the first was the worst because I fought back. I tried to push her away and yelled at her. She gets mad when I show my emotions.

So I stay loose like a rag doll and let her hit. First it's the face, then the ribs. I'm on the ground. She only grunts when she's letting loose her kicks. I can feel myself bruising. I blank out for minutes. I think she is done. But suddenly she bends down, grabs my hair and throws me into the shower stall. Hot water streams down on me. She hits my head against the shower wall before leaving.

Finally I let out my pain. I cry to my heart's content, biting on my arm so I won't let any sound out. Still in the shower, I slowly take off my jeans, baby blue button down shirt and socks and pile them at the far corner of the square shower so they won't get the bathroom floor wet. I then reach my hand out of the shower, dig under the towel shelf, and feel around for the box cutter I have hidden there for times like these. I start to cut my thigh and then my arm. I watch the blood from my thigh and arm go down the drain along with my tears and shower water, wishing I could wake up from this nightmare I call life.

A Note from Angel

I'm eighteen now and have been in foster care since my fifteenth birthday. I have been clean for three years. I did talk to my mom every now and then before she passed away in 2011. When I read Scriber's first book *We Are Absolutely Not Okay*, the stories reminded me a lot of my past. I wanted to write this story because I didn't want to keep it in any longer. After attending Scriber Lake for two weeks in the fall, I moved back to Arizona because I missed the sun. Marjie and I emailed nine drafts of this story back and forth and it has helped me come to terms with my past. I want to go to college and major in nursing.

IT'S BECAUSE WE LOVE YOU

KRISTINA EDGAR

I'm just a normal girl, lying in a pile of sins, wrapping myself in pain, covered in more than just another mistake and simple regret. I go to Scriber Lake High School. I have a boyfriend, Jesse, who kisses me every time he sees me and who holds my hand without hesitation.

I have a small circle of friends who wouldn't just leave me in the cold, lying on rocks, surrounded by grass. Most of all, I know that Jesse would have carried me to safe ground. But the thing is, he isn't here to save me tonight.

I am looking up at trees. I see wonderfully painted dark blue coats of empty sky, but no signs of life. I don't hear people or cars. A gust of wind makes its way through my thighs. I take a deep breath, trying to shake off the goose bumps that have made their way to the surface of my cold skin. I taste leftover alcohol.

My brain tells me to stand up, but I'm paralyzed with terror.

Where am I?

Rocks stab holes into the small of my bare back. I don't have any clue why I'm here or why my pants aren't on me. With each move that I try to make, I find another muscle that aches, sending more shocks through my nerves. A flow of anger bursts through my fingertips. I want to scream, but who will hear me if I do?

Why can't I sit up?

I slowly work my 185 pounds over to lie on my stomach. I feel heavy, but light at the same time. I look around and see no way to get out of this circular maze of grass, dirt, and dead leaves. *What have the trees witnessed?* I struggle to lift myself up, but I feel unconnected to my own body. I roll over onto my back, losing the motivation to get up.

"This is all a dream, Kristina," I say out loud.

I want someone to hear me. I keep saying, "It's all a terrible dream, you'll wake up from it. Just keep moving." But each time I try to move, I lose my balance.

"Fuck my life! Why are you doing this to me?" I scream at the sky.

I look up for a glimpse of light or an image of God.

I continue to look into the dark abyss, waiting for someone to come to my rescue. Minutes pass, they feel like hours; still no one comes.

Tears flow down the sides of my face into my ears. It tickles. I gaze into the clouds, but the sky seems so hollow, showing me no sign of someone or something that is going to guide me out of this dark, lonely place.

No one knows I'm here. My friends are at home, probably in bed. I'm sure my mom is worried, but she's no longer scared because it's a normal routine for me to tell her I'm going to be home at an agreed-upon time, and then not show up until hours later. It's normal for me to not come home.

If she only knew.

I roll over again to get onto my stomach, then pull myself up into a kneeling position—my butt touching the back of my legs. I'm in a perfect position to pray. I've forgotten how to, though. I'm all out of practice. I haven't done it in so long. But here goes nothing.

"Dear Lord," I speak slowly, with an even tone, allowing the smooth words to linger in the wind. "I know that I have failed you, failed to do my duties as your child. But I need you now more than ever. I need the strength to keep going. I need your help to show me what I need to do because I can't do it on my own. I know that I have said terrible things, and done worse. But you know just as well as I do that I can't just stay here."

I wait for another sign.

"Please, God, I know you hear me," I plead.

My mind fills with simple memories: time spent with my boyfriend, me crying on my best friend's shoulder, an 'I love you' spoken from my mom. Something in my chest eases and the heaviness lifts from me. I can't explain it—it doesn't feel supernatural or anything. It feels like getting out of a pool and stepping onto the cement when the sun is shining. I take a deep breath and a feeling of comfort rushes over my body.

My pants still aren't pulled up.

I have this odd feeling in my stomach, like I'm nervous. Like I've told a lie and I'm scared of getting caught. So I push it down further, to the pit of my stomach. That's the feeling my body has. My thighs are sore—everything is sore for that matter. I'm finally able to push up onto my bare feet, but a sharp pain shoots through my foot. A pinecone has made its way through my skin. I lean against the nearest tree to gain my balance from my shaking legs and wounded foot.

Both my legs are now in one large hole of my grey sweat pants, so I lift my right leg out to put it into its own slot. I tighten my drawstring to them hold up.

I now see a small, deep hole in my foot. To shake off my frustration, I kick the pinecone with the same foot it injured.

I look around to find my things. I don't know where I could have left my shoes. I know I had them. My legs feel like Jell-O, trying to hold up my weight. I lightly dust the small rocks off my lower back, amazed that I've accomplished so much. I feel the small dents in my skin where the rocks were. I pull my sweatshirt down because my whole tummy was exposed to the cold air.

I feel like I'm in a strobe light—every move is choppy. I finally see where the branches are a little thinner and spot a narrow path.

I walk out of the branches onto a cement path and see apartment buildings on the other side of a line of tall fir trees. The air smells like barbeque smoke mixed with that musty smell right before it rains. I have two choices: to go left or to go right. I have no idea how to get home; I don't even know what city I'm in.

Ennie, meenie, minie, mo. Left it is.

Walking down the trail, I listen. For anything. Birds, cars, lighters—anything. I continue to walk for five minutes until I am on a busy road. It looks familiar, but I can't quite place the scene. My brain is racing. I hesitate.

What If my parents see me? Will they be mad? Will they find out about what happened? Will they forgive me? Will they understand about the pain I felt lying there?

Things are still choppy; my legs move but I don't feel like I'm going anywhere. I turn right to walk down a steep hill and hear more signs of life. I get to the end of the trail and onto a main road. A police officer drives past. Shoreline Police. I look at him, but he's staring straight into his computer.

I am scared to ask him, "Can you please take me to my mom? I woke up with my pants down and now I don't know where to go from here."

So I continue to walk down the steep hill until I see a large mural on my side of the street next to an intersection. It features a group of kids of different races holding hands under a sun. Diagonally across the street is a familiar gas station. It's one I have gone to several times with my Nana to get small snacks and Arizona Teas when we take my brother and sister to the park. I finally know where I am. I cross the street and continue up a hill to get to the transit center.

When I finally get there, my bare, wounded feet are beyond sore. My goal is to find a phone to call my mother. If I can't find one, I'll have to walk all the way home.

I see an older woman who has just finished a conversation on her cell phone. She has long, stringy, dark brown hair. It's straight, parted down the center and really tangled. She looks like she hasn't brushed her teeth in a while or slept in at least a few days. But she is all I have right now.

"Excuse me, ma'am, may I use your phone to call my mother?" I ask her, sweetly.

"You slut!" she screams. "You smell like alcohol! Why would I let you use my phone?"

I'm in shock. I can't believe the way my heart feels; it has shattered in my chest. I just smile, though, and walk away, even though I want to beat her to the ground. I guess my journey home is going to continue from here.

I walk past the marijuana dispensary on Highway 99, smelling the aroma and looking at all the lights, absorbing everything I can. I have walked up this hill more a thousand times: sober, drunk and high. But this time, I feel that with each step, more of who I am falls in pieces behind me. Instead of walking the route I usually take, I think that if I just walk straight past the light that I might end up near my house. I drag myself across the road, pushing forward. I walk all the way down another street, but find out it's a cul de sac. I need to sit down, so I sit in someone's yard. The grass is so soft, perfect grass-pulling grass. It's smooth between my fingers. I just want to sit and close my eyes. I sit for about five minutes until a man and a woman pull into the driveway in a large, silver car. They look at me skeptically when they get out and slowly walk toward me. I just smile at them. I can only imagine how this looks.

"Can I use your phone to call my mama? I have had a shitty night. I just want to go home," I say, conscious of their stares. "Have you been drinking?" the tall man asks.

"Yes. I don't want any trouble. I just want to go the fuck home," I say. I don't mean to seem so irritated, but my body wants to shut down. They hand me a phone with no further questions and I dial my mother's number. I stare at the numbers and listen to it ring for what seems like forever.

"Hello?" my mom says with a pure, sleepy voice. It sends chills down my spine because I know that it may change by the end of this phone call.

"Mommy? I need you … I need you to come get me. I know that you're mad, but I need you to come get me now," I say, painfully.

"Do you know what time it is, Kristina Mae?"

There it is, the first and middle name. I'm in so much trouble.

"Yes, it's ten-thirty, Mama, I'm so sorry. But please, I'll explain everything when you get here. Please," I say, panicked that she might say "no."

"Where are you?"

"I don't know. I'll ask the people that let me use their phone."

"I have no idea where I am, will you please tell her?" I ask the man. "Yeah, no problem," he answers. He looks like he's in his late 20s and his facial blemishes show from the dim front porch light. He takes the phone from me, not looking me in the eye. He walks away with the phone. The woman walks over with hesitation; they both seem scared of me. I understand that I don't smell that great and that I have small fragments of grass and dirt in the knots of my ponytail. But I'm not a foreign being.

"You drank a lot, didn't you?" she says lightly. She's petite and younger than the man. Her hair is short; causing some pieces to come loose from her ponytail.

"Something like that," I grunt. "Can I have a cigarette, please?"

"Yes, you can. Would you like a water, too?"

I nod.

She walks over to the man, who is still on the phone with my mother. They return together. He gives me a cigarette and the phone, and she hands me a Fred Meyer bottled water. It's so cold.

"Kristina, I will be there in a few minutes. Be ready," my mom tells me.

"Okay, I love you," I say.

She hangs up.

"Do you need a lighter?" he asks.

"Yes, thank you."

The first drag I take is so sweet it gives me goose bumps. We don't talk much; they just sit and watch over me as I smoke my cigarette.

"Thank you so much. I wish you understood how much this means."

"It's just a cigarette," she says with a smile.

My mother and step-dad finally pull up to the house. I have never been so excited to see my parents in my entire life.

My mother gets out of the car and my step-father follows.

"Get in the truck," she says with a stern tone. Her dirty blonde hair is pulled into a flat bun and she's wearing black sweat shorts. Clearly, they have come straight from bed.

It's so warm in the truck. I watch the four of them talk for a minute before my parents return to the truck. The couple waves to me and I wave back.

"What the fuck happened? You smell like alcohol," my mother says.

I explain how I had drunk a little, and that I didn't remember falling asleep. How I woke up with my pants down in an area that I didn't recognize. How I found the couple and called them as soon as I could.

After I explain my night, they go silent.

"I'm sorry mommy, I'm so sorry." She stares at my step-dad, but he doesn't look back at her.

"We have to take you to the hospital, Kristina. If anything happened, we need to make sure that you are okay," he says in an even tone. He never shows his emotions to anyone but my mother.

"No! I'm fine! I just want to go home and shower!" I scream. My mom starts to cry.

"No, Kristina, you aren't fine. We need to take you to the hospital now," Todd says again.

"If you love me you won't take me to the hospital, you'll just take me home!" I cry. I can't believe this night might not be over.

After a long pause, Todd says, "No, Kristina, it's because we love you that we are taking you there."

My parents continue talking, but all I can hear is my own voice screaming inside of me, not wanting to know what happened. I just want to go home and sleep forever. I've stopped breathing and I feel really light-headed.

The minutes seem like hours as they drive toward the hospital. Finally I sink back into the seat and prepare to deal with the choice they have made for me.

A Note from Kristina

We ended up going to Swedish Hospital that night and my worst fear was confirmed after I was given a rape kit test. It has been almost a year since that night, and I am now clean from everything; I've even quit smoking cigarettes. I feel so much healthier! Today I'm working at a daycare and have earned my GED. I'm also getting involved with the Teal Lotus Project, based out of Cozad, Nebraska. This project helps people cope with the aftermath of sexual abuse. I plan to travel with them to schools, churches, and colleges to share my story, talk about prevention and coping skills, and encourage healthier lifestyles. http://theteallotusproject.com. I have battled sexual abuse my whole life. The best advice I can give to anyone who has been in my shoes is to keep going and not let the pain rule your life. It will ruin your everyday choices, affect the way you treat people and even how you choose to love another person. Don't let predators rule you; don't let them win. If you or anyone you know has battled with sexual abuse, speak up and tell the police. Also, get professional treatment. You deserve more. You're worth it. It's not too late! Thank you for reading my story.

NEVER TOO LATE

JACQUIE LAMPIGNANO

The classroom is quiet and the lights are dimmed as we work in our Spanish textbooks. I can't hear anything but flipping pages and whispers as my classmates keep their voices low so the teacher won't hear. Because there are only fifteen minutes left in class, I am barely working; concentrating on the slow steady tick of the clock above the door. I feel a low buzz and see a dim glow from below the desk. My phone is vibrating.

I reach into the pocket of my jeans to pull it out and turn it off. This class is horrendous for texting. The teacher is known to have x-ray vision and is willing to take every cell phone she spots. I'm about to hit the power button when I glance at the screen. It's McCaela. My best friend. She knows I'm in class. Why is she texting me now?

I glance across the room and take a quick peek at the teacher's desk. She's working on something and won't notice if I look at the text really quickly. I take the risk and press the cold enter button.

"I'm sorry and I love you," reads the message. My heart instantly jolts and I feel a cold shiver go down my spine. "What did you do?" I respond quickly.

I think about the conversation we had an hour earlier. I was sitting at a table in the commons area before class started, mingling with my fellow sixteen hundred students. I go to Lynnwood High while McCaela attends Scriber. Previously a Lynnwood Royal, McCaela transferred schools to better herself and her education. My phone had rung and I happily answered, excited to hear the voice of my best friend. She was upset, unlike her natural happy demeanor. She explained that she and her boyfriend had broken up. I think she loved him. I tried my best to cheer her up, but with the limited time before class started I couldn't really do much to help. My phone buzzes again. I take it out and look at the screen.

"I took 64 Vicodin. I'm so sorry."

I read the message. I reread the message. My body turns to stone and my hands become clammy as I hold the cold metal phone, which is slowly becoming warmer as my flesh turns to ice. *What is she thinking?!* I push the chair away roughly so that it bangs into the desk behind me. I briskly walk to the teacher's desk. *My best friend is thinking about ending her life and I'm stuck in this tedious class,* is all that is swimming through my mind.

May I use the restroom? I practically bark at her in my rush to escape this classroom that is caving in around me.

She barely looks at me as she nods. I rush to the bathroom. *"Please, please don't do this,"* I'm screaming to myself as I run into a stall. I bolt myself in and dial McCaela's number. Thankfully it's early in the morning so there is nobody in the bathroom. As the phone rings my heart swells in my chest and starts beating at ten times the normal rate; so fast it feels like it's going to beat out of my chest.

"Hey everybody, it's me, McCaela. I can't come to the phone right now..." I cut off her voicemail before it has time to end. I start calling again and again. No answer. How can this be happening? I love her so much and so do so many other people. How can she think this is the only way out? That she doesn't have so many other people supporting her?

Five minutes left in class. I float back to class because I can't think. I feel like a ghost. I'm trying with all my might to contain myself even though it feels like a part of me is being viciously torn out, stomped on and then burned. I grab my backpack and walk back to the door to wait for the bell. I might try to explain it to any other teacher, but I am on the verge of a meltdown and I doubt she will understand the situation if I try to explain.

Two minutes left in class. Why McCaela? Why are you doing this? I understand you are hurt, but how could you do this to your mom who adores you? To all your friends who would be devastated? To Jake who would lose yet another sibling to suicide?

Two years ago, McCaela's older brother Josh killed himself. It was our freshman year and it was the same as any other week. McCaela, Ashleigh, and I were sitting in Biology together on the wobbly stools around our lab table. McCaela told us how Josh had been gone for a few days.

"He's eighteen. He's probably just being a typical teenager and will come back home any day now," I had reassured her.

He didn't come back, though, and McCaela wasn't at school the next day. Josh was found dead after lighting a mini grill and letting the gas fill up his car. He died from carbon monoxide poisoning. Her heartbreak had been of astronomical proportions. Earlier that same year, during our "If I Dressed Like This, Would You Still Be My Friend?" spirit theme day, McCaela had dressed up as Josh. She had worn his jeans, shirt, and boxers. She idolized her big brother.

One minute left in class. My body starts sputtering in my efforts to keep my tears in. Everybody around me is laughing, so deep in their own worlds—not knowing that somebody out there, somebody I care about so much, is trying to kill herself. I could practically be part of the wallpaper I am so not in the moment.

The bell finally rings. I run out of the room into the long hallway and as I do the floodgates release. Tears blur my vision. Not just small tears, tears that literally feel like they could give water to children of Africa for a week. It feels like no matter how fast I am going, I'm not going to make it to the end of the hallway. I'm not going to make it in time to save her. *What if she is dying right now? What if she is seizing because of how much toxic waste she forced through her system?* All these what-ifs are going through my head. I finally make it out of the hallway after what seems like a million years. Out of the hallway down the stairs in the middle of the common area past the Ala Carte to the counseling office doors.

I walk into the office, face drenched with tears. The secretary looks at me and immediately asks, "What's wrong?"

"My friend is trying to kill herself," I blubber, because that is all I can do. My body is so grief-stricken that I've gone into convulsions. She bolts out of her seat and leads me to a counselor. He is seated behind his desk and as I enter he turns to look at me. With the way my face looks, covered with tears and snot dripping down my lips, someone might assume that someone had died. He also asks me what's wrong. I explain the situation and his attention is fully on me.

"Is your friend a student here?" he asks.

"No, but she used to be. She goes to Scriber Lake now; her younger brother is a student here," I respond, still blubbering.

He tells me that they probably still have her record on file and looks up her name on his computer. As he pulls it up I can see her picture on the screen. Her hair is still its natural dirty blonde and she has a round full face that enhances the roundness of her dimples. She has beautiful big blue eyes. I look at the picture and feel rage take over me.

"You couldn't just talk to me?" I want to scream at her. "You couldn't call your mom? You couldn't wait fifty minutes to talk to me again? Does Jake not matter? Do you want to leave him sibling-less, an only child if you also choose to kill yourself? Do all of your friends not matter? You are going to let one boy control your decision on whether or not you live?"

The counselor picks up the phone and calls our school's liaison officer and tells her what is happening. He turns to me and says, "She is driving over to her house to see if she is still there and if she needs help." At this point I'm shaking but at least my tears are drying into wet trails on my face. He stares at me for a second and asks me if I'm okay.

Do I look okay? My best friend, the person I turn to when my own fits of depression are going haywire, is trying to kill herself.

Both McCaela and I deal with depression and have problems with cutting, but we know that whenever something is wrong we can come to each other. I can remember many late night conversations when I've been at my very worst and she has brought me back from that deep dark hole.

I tell him I am fine.

The next call is to Scriber. He explains what I've told him: that one of their students is trying to commit suicide. My ears try to grasp as much of the conversation as I can.

"Oh, she's there," he says and his eyes dart to me. What follows is a mixture of "yesses" and muttered "mm-hmms." Then he hangs up and spins his chair to face me. His chair is taller than the one I am sitting in and the way he looks at me, it sort of feels like he is a judge about to give me a death sentence. Not my own but one for a person I care about, which hurts more than if it was my own. How many people can say they would die for the ones they love? I know I would. I would do anything to trade my life to save McCaela.

"McCaela is at school and they have pulled her out of class," he says. "She is in the office throwing up. They have called an ambulance and her mother, who is on her way to the hospital."

I breathe a sigh of relief. I didn't realize it but the whole time I had been holding my breath. I was thinking how I was going to live without her, and how I would have to go to all my other friends and try to get them to understand that joke that only she understood. About how there would be no more awesome memories spent at her house or walking around the park right down the street, and about how all my memories would be tainted with a sad cloud because she would no longer be with me. I felt like a huge boulder had been lifted off my shoulders. The responsibility was no longer just on me. I did the best I could to get her help and now she was being taking care of.

The tears strike up again. Not tears of sadness, but tears of happiness. I look down at my dirty, beat-up Converse tennis shoes. Through my tears I smile and laugh. It is all I can think of to do.

"I told Scriber that we would like updates," he says. "So if you want to come by the rest of the day to check up, that would be fine. Would you like to stay here or go back to class?"

I glance up and say, "I think I can make it to class." He writes me a note as I sling my bag over my shoulder. I walk out the door to the waiting area, where I decide to sit for a while to compose myself. I feel physically drained of all emotion.

As I walk into my next class more than half an hour late, everybody is busy studying for our upcoming history test. It seems almost surreal that normal life has been going on after what I have been through. I hand the pass to my teacher, walk quietly to my seat and try to wind myself back into a normal day.

A Note from Jacquie

It has been two years since I saved my best friend's life. Because of the phone call that was made to Scriber, the ambulance took her to Swedish Edmonds in time for her stomach to get pumped. Last spring I watched McCaela get her diploma and I felt so proud of her. After the ceremony

I was talking to her mother and she told me how grateful she was and how her daughter would not be there if it weren't for me. I have watched my best friend become an inspiration for others, speaking out against bullying and about suicide prevention while telling her story and that of her brother. It can be as simple as standing up for that kid you have never talked to or saying a friendly word to someone who seems like they are having a bad day, but I believe everybody can wear the cape of a superhero for someone. About a month after McCaela's suicide attempt, I myself tried to commit suicide, but with the help of friends, I pulled through. I finished out the year at Lynnwood and switched to Scriber to get away from the stress and triggers and to have a fresh start. This spring I will be graduating. I can't say I am completely better, but I can say it has gotten easier. I am now the editor of my yearbook, I have an amazing girlfriend, and I have a great support network of friends. After high school I hope to either pursue professional photography or directing. It is true what everybody says: life does get better. The problems that are tormenting you now will seem miniscule ten years from now. I hope that by sharing this story, others will realize that they can be that person who saves a life. It only takes one friend to save someone.

MAN-MAN

LADAWN HARRIS

BAM! BAM! BAM! The pounding of drums beat over and over. A shadow is cast about this room. Only the faint flickering of small medieval torches hinged to the walls illuminate the dainty path in front of me. Each blow to the goatskin sends vibrations to my feet, transmitting to my fingertips.

BAM! BAM! BAM! I snap out of my dream and realize that the beat is actually someone pounding on the front door. Not just *someone*, a cop. Who else could it be at two in the morning? Plus, cops have a distinctive kind of knock. One that says, "I am in charge and you will open up. Now!" Their knocks are always hard and continuous.

I open my eyes to the darkness of my room. I prop myself up in my bed, waiting and listening. I hear the creaking of steps and the railing buckle slightly as someone descends the stairs. The metal hook-like stands that hold up the railing have become loose from years of aggressive treatment, and now creak whenever the railing is touched.

I peek outside my balcony to see red and blue lights flashing around our townhouse parking lot. They shine on a multitude of cars, trees and finally through to my room as I pull back the soft zebra-striped blanket I have hanging for a curtain.

I can barely make out the discussion, though I overhear the words, "Antonio Carter." Then I hear a male police officer's voice say, "Car accident."

Oh my God. My brother! I know only two Antonio Carters; one of them is my dad, who is here. Fear, regret and realization collide in my brain. My mind locks on the repeated phone calls I received from my sister the night before. I should have answered, but I was thinking of myself and how I wanted to sleep. When we talk, it's always for a while. I knew I would be on the phone for too long. Not that I don't love talking to my sister, I just have to have the time for it.

I quickly search for my phone. I feel the answer is there before I even know what the question is.

The first message reads, "Man Man's unconscious."

The second one reads, "Man Man's dead."

I feel my stomach churn and knot up. *Why hadn't I answered the phone? Why had I been so selfish?* I wasn't thinking that if I answered my phone that could be the last time that I would have a brother. I wasn't thinking about all the things that I had yet to talk to him about, the places around the world we had yet to travel, or riches and fame we had yet to achieve as thespians, models and entrepreneurs. Not me. I was thinking of myself.

I freeze. Pause. Stop. Stare. A new feeling of numbness sinks in. I just sit, trying to make sense of what I have just read. I read the messages over and over to make sure this is actually happening. Even though I know what has happened, I refuse to believe it. *Maybe he's still unconscious. Maybe she just thinks that he's dead. He's probably just on a machine and he's not responding. He's going to be okay.*

I hear my dad shut the door. Hard footsteps slowly ascend the stairs.

"What's wrong? What happened?" It's my mom. Her voice sounds panicked and scared.

"Man-Man was in a car accident," I hear him tell her. Each word my dad speaks carries the weight of the world. My mom becomes frantic, pacing and squealing.

I overhear my dad tell her that my brother is at Harborview Medical Center. My sisters, their mom, grandma and aunts and uncles are there already.

"Get ready," is all he says as he stops by my door. These words are solid and cold. My dad and I quickly get dressed and jump in the car for the forty-five minute drive to Seattle. My mom, who is Man-Man's step-mom, has recently landed a job after being unemployed for more than a year. In a few hours she will start her second day. She's worried about what her employer will think if she asks for the day off, so she decides to stay home.

I don't tell my parents about the second message my sister sent. I tell them that my brother is unconscious, but not that he is dead. I don't know that they have both received the texts as well. I guess none of us can admit it to ourselves, let alone to each other.

Lost in my thoughts, I realize we are driving through the misty fog on I-5 at three in the morning. I want to say something to my dad, but we both stay silent. There is nothing to say. Words will only add to the confusion. We remain frozen and numb, attempting to process what is going on, not knowing what to expect. What is there to do or say when you know you will never see your friend, brother or son again?

We begin to enter a familiar tunnel. Only today, this tunnel isn't a checkpoint for the usual fun adventures that Seattle holds. No, today this tunnel feels like a trap. It's like we are about to enter a dungeon. We are just getting closer and closer to something awful.

When we arrive at the hospital, I call my sister and ask her where she is.

"I'm waiting outside the ER," she says in a monotone voice.

"Okay." A solemn fragment of a sentence is all I can manage.

Nearing the emergency room entrance, I spot my sister standing with our aunt. Nicotine smoke fills the dark sky with every exhale of her cigarette. The visual of this is somewhat calming, but anything at this point can be analyzed as having beauty. All the things I could have done and should have done run through my head. Things I had not yet said to my brother or done for him to show my appreciation for all the things he's done for me. The beauty in just being alive has new meaning.

When the cigarette is out, I feel the worst because now it's time to face death. Walking through the never-ending hallway, my vision becomes blurred around my peripheral and I become focused. Focused on keeping calm, on trying to prepare myself for something that no one is prepared for.

Before we enter the room, I take a deep breath. The confidence I had tried to convince myself I have has completely vanished. I am now whimpering, hesitantly taking steps towards the room. I see bodies huddled in the far corner of the room, surrounding the bed that holds my brother. There is an empty bed to the left of his bed. A curtain hangs, separating the two. When I step closer, my step-grandma hugs me, squeezing tighter than ever. This is followed by hugs from my step-mom and my sister. Then they clear the way for me to see my brother.

There are no machines. There is no longer an IV. There is no life. There is only death. A tube with some sort of plastic breathing device is still lodged down my brother's throat. I want to rip it out so he can breathe. His body is a very pale, light brown. Close to a skin shade he would have admired, though his face is tinted with yellow. His left eye is big and purple. The muscles in his face are too relaxed, causing his eyes to spread underneath the thin surface of his eyelids. The hairs in his nose are tipped and slightly clumped with blood. I kiss his cheek and rest mine on his. I hold his hands, squeezing them gently, wanting so badly for my hands to heat his up.

His body is usually so muscular, but now he is extremely stiff. Not solid and exuberant, but hard and freezing. His face and left arm are the only parts of him exposed because of the extreme mutilation he has suffered. The blanket is supposed to protect us from mentally torturing ourselves with an image that we will never be able to erase.

His body, mind, heart and soul are gone. We are all crying, praying, yelling and staring. I just want him to wake up—we all do. In between sobs my sister Tionna begs, "Wake up! Wake up! Please!" But he doesn't.

A new sense fills the room, as if his spirit is standing next to me, seeing what we see.

After a few minutes, we all leave. Stepping out into the cold, bittersweet early morning air allows my blood to flow more easily. The anxiety begins to diminish, and again I am able to think. Our family says our goodbyes and we go our separate ways.

Back in the car, my dad and I cry. He rests his hand on the middle seat of his white 1990 Cadillac Deville. The interior has beige-khaki colored leather seats and cream-colored carpet. All I can do is stare blankly and think about my brother. The date is September 25th, 2012. It's 5 a.m. and the sun is already beginning to show itself. There are no clouds in the sky. It's beautiful. It seems so wrong for the sun to appear, acting as if nothing has happened. Maybe it's my brother's spirit.

My brother Antonio—who our family called Man-Man—wanted to live forever. He was constantly overcoming past mistakes in his life so he could better his future. He went from smoking weed, drinking and failing his classes to getting all A's. He had enrolled in Running Start so that he could finish high school, then attended Highline Community College and Bellevue College. He was able to obtain free lifeguarding lessons over the summer and landed a job as a lifeguard at the Bellevue Club. His next job was working at UPS, making sixteen dollars an hour. He was so motivated and never settled. If something wasn't good enough, he did whatever he needed to do to change it. I always wished I could be like him. He was only a year and six days older than me—born August 3, 1994.

Man-Man taught himself Russian and Japanese through the help of one of his Russian friends and a Japanese book my mom bought for me. I ended up giving it to him because I gave up. But he never did. He even attempted to teach me, but being the procrastinator that I am, I couldn't do it. I could remember how to say, 'I love you' in Russian and Japanese, and could count to twenty-nine in Japanese without having to think about it. But Man-Man constantly spoke it to our family, even though we couldn't understand what he was saying. It was always so amazing hearing the foreign jargon spill out of his mouth, and seeing him study for hours.

We were so similar, yet so different. When he thought about something, he would make this sound where he exhaled a swift," shtuu shtuu shtuu" noise. Whenever we were together, we would talk, like TALK, for hours. I've never had that connection with anyone else, or the ability to continuously talk for hours about both constructive and random things.

If you had seen Antonio walking down the street, you would noticed his confidence—it came through in every step he took. He wanted to be a model and definitely had the look and walk for it. Man-Man was so well-groomed. He always shaved his head and face and always dressed nice. He usually wore three-hundred dollar Red Monkey jeans, a new pair of DC's, an Abercrombie V-neck, a white North Face jacket and a black flapper hat with brown or grey fuzz. He would either smell like Phoenix Axe Spray or Jean Paul Gaultier's 'La Male', a beautiful scent that comes in a blue-striped bottle shaped in the physique of a man.

It strikes me as funny that despite how beyond intelligent my brother was, his geography was questionable. I recall him denying that Alaska was a part of the United States. I couldn't believe it, but that is one of my many treasured memories of my brother.

Antonio Carnate Carter Jr. had so many goals and plans for his future and was in the process of realizing them all. I would later find out how my brother died. He had been street racing against a man who ran him off the road, sending his car spinning into the curb. Man-Man had been driving so fast that the force from hitting the curb sent the car flying about ten feet in the air before slamming into a massive tree. My sister told me that the dude who ran him off the road yelled, "That's what you get, fucker!" I have no words for that comment. It hurts too much to think about.

My dad's sobs interrupt my thoughts and bring me back to the car. Only yesterday I had two Antonios in my life. Now we both have only one. We sit in the car, crying. No words are said, only hugging and crying. Now it's time to live a new life: one where I don't have a brother, and my dad doesn't have a son.

A Note from LaDawn

Seven months later, I still cannot believe that my brother is gone—even though spiritually he is still here. It's been a struggle to wear a smile on my face every day, but for the most part I can manage. I still think about Man-Man every day, and his memory motivates me to be better. I admire him so much because of his incredible determination. Feeling him with me pushes me along. At first, I felt like giving up. I no longer had the glimpse of motivation that allowed me to get through school; I was done. I stayed in bed all day crying for a few weeks before I was able to start healing. After returning to school, I made the decision to transfer to Scriber Lake High School. I am a person who believes in fate and destiny for both the negative and positive aspects in life. If I had not transferred schools, my brother's story may have never been heard. Psychology, neurobiology and becoming an actress inspire me to graduate high school and continue to college. I would love to attend the University of Washington because my mom graduated from there. I still have obstacles to conquer, but the challenges get a little bit easier every day. I know that if I stay motivated, I can overcome anything.

STREET LIFE

CHRISTOPHER MILBRAD

"Shit!" my friend yelled as loud as he possibly could. "Chris, the cops are here!"

I had been staying at my friend's house for approximately two weeks, sleeping on the floor of his parents' bedroom. I was totally engrossed in rolling a cigarette with paper and a two-inch line of tobacco. I had been attempting this for weeks and still couldn't do it. So when my friend yelled, it didn't even register for a good ten seconds.

"What do you mean the cops are here?" I yelled back after I finally got a grip on reality. "You better not be fucking with me right now! I swear I will kick your ass!"

I was flipping out because I had been reported as a runaway again. If I was caught, I knew I would be sent to juvenile detention. I didn't want to go. I had already spent six weeks there.

A year earlier, my mom approached me as I sat on the couch, engaged in my favorite TV show, "Rob and Big."

"Christopher, there is something I need to talk to you about," she said with a flat, serious tone. "I lost my job today, which means we won't have very much money. So we are going to have to live in a motel for a little while."

It took me a good minute to process this information. I basically didn't say anything back to her. I just sat there watching my show and thinking, *What the fuck?* This was something that I never thought would happen. Not in a million years. For twenty-five years, my mom had steady work as a paralegal.

That's when my life took a turn for the worse. Not long after, we moved into a small, rundown, $35-a-night motel room. The main office was dingy and dark and smelled of cigarette smoke and stale coffee. The outside light flickered constantly.

The room we stayed in was even crappier than the main office. It was on the second floor where all of the walls were dark yellow because of smoke, even though neither of us smoked at the time.

The door to our room looked like it had been painted red twenty years ago. It was green before, so with the chipped paint, the door was now both red and green. There was only one old creaky bed, so I slept on the floor. The flat carpet had a thin layer of dirt across it so it was a dingy, grayish brown. If you slapped it, dust would fly. Steel bars covered our one window. There was a mini-fridge, a small microwave and a sink. The bathroom was the smallest I had ever seen. This motel room was definitely not big enough for two people.

Living in a motel sucked like crazy because at the time I wasn't attending school. My mom was so stressed trying to find a job and figure out ways to get money that she never had time to enroll me in school. I would wake up, go to the bathroom and turn on the TV. I would watch cartoons and eat Top Ramen, juice and cereal. I started getting creative and put butter and Ranch dressing in the Top Ramen to make it taste better, which didn't help my health much.

After about a month of not going to school and sitting around all day, I expressed my feelings about it—in a bad way—to my mom.

"Mom! I fucking hate sitting around here doing nothing!" I yelled.

By the next week I was enrolled in a high school that was just three blocks from the motel. I started attending ninth grade regularly.

Everything was going fine. But after a while there was this one guy who was a straight ass to me every day, every single chance he got, even though I had known him for a long time and we had never had problems. One day he embarrassed me to an extreme in front of all of my new friends. He knew things about me from middle school that no one else did.

"Do you guys know this kid still has to wear diapers when he sleeps?" he yelled. All I could do was just walk away, thinking about what my friends thought of me after that asshole guy told them that. It was something that wasn't even true anymore.

The worst thing was that I never did anything about it and neither did anyone else. I didn't try to fight him and I never defended myself. But my day of humiliation and frustration wasn't over. After school and all this other stuff that had gone down, I had to deal with more shit.

"CHRISTOPHER! I told you to clean the mouse cage three days ago! Yet you still haven't done it!" my mom barked at me as soon as I walked in the door.

All these things had just been adding up day after day, same shit different day—until I finally couldn't take it anymore. I made a decision to run away forever and live my life somewhere else—without school or my mom. I thought this would be best for me.

That day was the day that I ran away from home for the first time. It only lasted for three days. I stayed at a friend's house for two days and walked around Seattle with a couple of my friends for another. A cop stopped us and I was arrested and put in juvenile detention for another three days. After that, whenever things got even a little bit tough, I resorted to running away.

The second time I ran away I was gone for two and a half months. It was a long time to be away from home. For the first week I stayed at a friend of a friend's house. It was fun while it lasted. It was all about drinking and smoking cigarettes. But that ended quickly when I got into a fight with one of the other people at the house. He kept walking all over the blankets and me while I was sleeping so I grabbed his head and smashed it against a wall. I thought that maybe I would teach him a lesson about stepping on people while they slept. Instead, two guys picked me up and threw me out the door.

For a couple of days I stayed under a bridge with some friends. It was terrible. Both nights it was raining, so our clothes got soaked. Both times I had to walk around all day with wet clothes on. Every night we had to find a church that served free food. It sucked.

But then I ran into one of my old, good friends. I told him my situation and he offered to let me stay with him as long as I needed. So that's what I did. I stayed with him for the rest of the two months that I was gone from home. I slept in his parents' bedroom on the floor. I had enough to eat, a TV, and people who cared about me.

Then one day the cops came to my friend's house looking for me. I tried to play it like I was someone else. But that didn't work at all and I was taken in to the police station. It was the worst having to deal with cops like that.

The third time I ran away from home was for only a month. Of course I went back to the same place where I had been caught the time before, but this time I was determined not to get caught. I was there for about a week and a half before the cops came again—right when I was trying to roll that cigarette.

"I mean the cops are right outside the house, right now!" my friend yelled again. Everything froze, me and everything else that was going on around me; it all stopped. I felt a sudden twinge in my stomach and immediately started sweating. My hands began to shake. Then I heard faint noises, almost as if there was someone outside screaming their head off. But then I realized the yelling was coming from right behind me.

"Hey, you! Snap out of it!" This time my friend wasn't just yelling. It was like a primal roar uttered from the deepest, darkest spot of his stomach, bubbling, waiting to come up, then finally bursting from between his lips.

I didn't see his hand coming toward my face, but I felt the hit like a Ping-Pong paddle. The sting of his slap got my attention. Finally, I snapped out of my dead trance and booked it down the hall, around the corner and out the back door. My friend's uncle, Torriano, happened to be standing there. He grabbed me. He was 6'6" and 280 pounds, and about ninety percent of that was muscle. He had deep brown eyes said, "I can kill you in an instant if I wanted to." He was probably the scariest person I have ever met, and if he told you to do something, you did it with high hopes that he wouldn't strangle the shit out of you.

"In the garage there are some rafters high up. If you can climb up onto them, you may have a chance at getting away," Tori said as he turned away, his hand still wrapped tightly around my arm. As he dragged me toward the garage door, I thought that this could be the end of my month-long adventure.

"By the way, you might want to keep the noise level to a minimum up there," he said with a laugh as we walked down the steps to the garage. He pointed to the rafters on which I would be laying. Tori always talked like he was joking, but when you looked at his face you knew he was dead serious about whatever it was that he said.

I heard the cops outside, knocking on the front door.

Shit! I scrambled clumsily up the short stack of wooden boxes that were sitting at the bottom of one of the poles. Just as I got all the way up on the thin beam—which was supposed to hold me up for I don't know how long—a short, stocky cop walked into the garage. My breath caught. I felt like he could hear my every heartbeat. The cop, who could easily put me away for a while if he caught me, made a full search of the whole garage. He looked in the trunk of Tori's car, under boxes, in boxes, under the bed and everywhere else he thought I could possibly be hiding.

The only place he didn't check was where I was: Up.

A Note from Chris

Two weeks later, another cop came. That time I was out in front of the house smoking a cigarette and had nowhere to hide. They took me in and gave me a week in juvenile detention. After I got out, I started going to counseling. During the time I was gone, my mom moved into a different motel in South Everett, slightly better but still bad. Eventually I ended up at the most amazing school I could have ever hoped for. I've done the best at Scriber Lake High School, and it's better than any other school. I'm still struggling a little bit, but I'm doing so much better. I'm headed to inpatient treatment in a couple of months. As soon as I finish that I'm going to start going back to Scriber so I can graduate. I'll be eighteen by the time I'm out of inpatient. I am going to get a job as soon as possible and hopefully get my own place.

AAABDAD

DELANIE HIGBEE

The light of my phone drew my eyes like the only light in a dark forest. I had no idea who would be texting me at two-thirty in the afternoon on a weekday. All of my friends were sitting around me on the school bus and could have easily spoken to me.

Curiosity getting the best of me, I slid my finger over the lock and saw it was from 'AaabDad.' I had put the a's and b's in front of 'Dad' so he would be at the top of my contact list. I wanted him to be easy to get to and always right there when I needed to ask or tell him something. But normally he didn't text me first, especially when he was at work.

Puzzled, I looked down at the screen and quickly clicked Read Now. I felt my cheeks get hot as I read the words. My eyes began to fill with tears but I dabbed them away before somebody saw. I turned to face the window, away from everyone around me. I was embarrassed and ashamed that I was about to cry. *How could life go so bad in only three days?*

❦

I was sitting in bed watching cartoons, the same as every Saturday morning, when I heard my mother yell for my brother and me to come downstairs for a family announcement.

It was still early for me so getting out of bed was the last thing I wanted to do. I reluctantly pulled myself out of bed, headed to the kitchen and sat down at our floating bar. My brother sat next to me and my mother was standing a few feet away. Her brown and blonde hair was flat and dull, like she had just gotten out of bed. She had a black house robe wrapped around her and she was wearing cheap glasses she called 'Cheaters.'

My eyes darted from her to my dad. He was sitting in a chair a few feet from my Mom and wouldn't make eye contact with any of us.

I felt a wave of panic wash over me because I had a pretty good idea of what the big deal was about. Not only had my big-mouthed mother told me this the day before, but it was truly obvious just by looking at my dad that he had a horrible announcement to make.

I was scared; I didn't want him to end the way of life I had been living so comfortably for twelve years.

My dad finally looked up at us, still avoiding my eyes. He touched his black mustache like he always did when he had something hard to say.

"I'm going to leave for a bit," he said in a calm, confident voice, as if he had practiced saying it in a mirror.

With every word he spoke, my heart sank lower and lower into my chest. He told us he would be moving out for a while and living in our motor home. He said he planned to stay at a campground in the area.

I couldn't imagine my dad leaving. He was what made us a family. I knew that if he left, everything would change for the worse. The house was already divided: my mother and her loving son against my dad and me. But now I was going to be left with no one on my side but myself. I didn't want anything to change. I was happy with the dysfunction as it was. I needed him here so he could be on my side and I wasn't alone. But I also knew that I loved him enough to let him leave if that's what he wanted. I wanted my dad to be happy and it was clear he wasn't happy with my mom. So if they needed a break, I thought it was a small price to pay to lose him for a while and have my family come back together eventually.

The room was dead silent before my mother spoke up. "Does anyone have any questions?" she asked, sounding like a teacher. "Lane?"

"No," I said quietly, trying to avoid her stare. I couldn't help but feel like this was all her fault. I wanted to cry because I was hurt, but I also wanted to scream at her because I felt like she wanted to hurt me. Like she wanted to take him away from me.

Deep down I knew it wasn't her fault. It was her nature to try to fix any problems in our family, but there was nothing my mom or anyone could do if she and Dad simply weren't in love anymore.

Even though I knew that, I still thought, *Maybe if you had loved him as much as I did he wouldn't be leaving us right now.*

No one said anything else. I knew my dad was feeling guilty, but I couldn't do or say anything. I wanted to hug him and tell him that I would be waiting for his return and that, no matter what, I would still love him. But I didn't want him to leave, so I pretended like he wasn't going to. I told myself I would just put it off until he actually left, which I figured wouldn't be for a while.

My dad stood up and left the room. With every footstep he took, I imagined him walking out of the house and out of my life. I tried to convince myself that one day he'd be back, but honestly I wasn't sure.

I looked back down at dad's message, studying every word. "I left today. I won't be far and I'll always be around for you. I love you, Trouble."

The bus was nearing my stop. I needed to pull myself together. I had planned to spend the afternoon at a friend's house, but I made an excuse and told her that I needed to go home. I preferred to spend the day at home alone than with her anyway. I really just used her for company and if that made her upset, it didn't really matter to me. At this point, nothing mattered.

I got off the bus and made the five-minute walk to my house. The first thing I noticed was the large, empty parking space where the RV once was. I almost didn't even recognize my house without it. Just like the empty space in front of my house, we now had an empty spot in our family. I didn't understand how he could just up and leave like that. I couldn't comprehend the fact that he was gone now.

I stepped onto the empty cement pad and then cut across my lawn to the entrance. I walked into my house feeling lonely and abandoned. I secretly wished my dad had waited for me to come home so he could have taken me with him. I knew life with him would be everything I wanted it to be. He was always the one who gave me freedom and gave me the option to choose what I wanted to do. I didn't want him missing out on half my childhood. He made us a family and had made our house a home. Without him, we were like strangers living together.

I phoned my mom, thinking she would comfort me.

"Mom," I said, choking on my words. "Dad's gone."

"Are you serious?" I could hear the anger in her voice. Her response surprised me. Apparently she didn't expect him to leave so soon, either.

"Yes, he told me almost twenty minutes ago," I practically whispered. I wanted her to tell me that everything was going to be okay, that she and Dad would work it out and that I had nothing to worry about. Instead she was quiet for a moment.

"Alright. Well, I'll be home soon," was all she said before hanging up.

I sat down on the couch in shock. My mother hadn't said anything to give me hope.

I looked at my phone and opened it to my dad's message. I had not yet responded. My heart was broken. There was so much I wanted to tell him. I wanted him to know that I wasn't angry that he left and I wanted to say that I needed him. I needed him to know that no matter what, I'd still be his daughter, a daughter who loved and appreciated him even if he didn't live with me. But I didn't want to make him feel any more guilt. So when I flipped my phone into full keyboard mode and texted him back, I kept my message short.

"I'll miss you," I typed, pausing to wipe the water flooding down my face. "Let me know when you're coming home. I love you too, Dad."

A Note from Delanie

My parents divorced in 2009. At this time I am currently living with my mom and our relationship continues to grow. I have realized that none of what happened was anybody's fault and I now know that my parents only want what's best for my brother and me. I'm a sophomore at Scriber Lake High School and I have bright plans for the future. I'm planning to pursue a career in writing and attend a four-year university (hopefully the UW!). I wanted to share my story because I personally needed this relief. I want other people to understand that sometimes divorce is the best option, and in some cases it can make everything better. Both of my parents are single and happy and I enjoy spending time with each of them. Right now I love my life and have some pretty amazing friends. They have helped me through a lot and I don't know where I'd be without them. Being a part of this book has been one of my best and most memorable high school experiences.

(Y)OU
(O)NLY
(L)IVE
(O)NCE

NATANAEL SANTAMARIA

"Bro, are you on your way now or what?" my friend Chupi asked, once again messaging me through Facebook. It was midnight and I had been lying in bed for what felt like hours, waiting for my parents to be fast asleep so I could escape with the car and go cruising with Chupi. I loved the fact that they were both heavy sleepers. Dad's heavy snoring made me love him even more. The only issue was getting them to actually go to sleep.

"Just wait, man! My parents aren't asleep yet!" I replied, listening to their muffled voices through my bedroom wall.

I knew it was getting late because of the comfortable and sleepy feeling I was getting. I was so relaxed I pretty much didn't want to leave any more. But I had already told Chupi I would be there and had things arranged.

After waiting for what felt like another hour, everything finally went quiet. Then I heard the signal I had been waiting for: Dad's snoring. It was time for my escape.

I quickly threw on a pair of jeans and a white hoodie. Then I shoved my five-foot pillow under my blankets to make it look like a sleeping body before tiptoeing out of my room and into the bathroom.

As I always did during my nightly escapes, I flipped on the bathroom fan, waited for a minute (which seemed like a hundred minutes) and then turned on the shower water. I often took long late-night showers before bed so it was a sound my parents were used to. I wanted to make as much noise as possible to block out the sound of the car engine when I started it.

With the fake shower in full swing, it was time for my next move.

I tiptoed from the bathroom to the top of the stairs, sat down and began to slide one stair at a time, as if going down a playground slide. I knew this is what I had to do because my stairs were extremely squeaky. I didn't want noise to ruin my plan.

Once I was finally at the bottom I headed to the kitchen, grabbed the car keys from the hook on the wall, slipped on my Nikes sitting near the front door and quietly made my way to the back sliding door. I always chose the slider door for my escape because I knew the front door would be far too complicated to open without making any noise.

That's when I saw him: my white fluffy dog, about the size of a soccer ball, lying inches from the sliding door in his kennel. Usually I remembered this part of my procedure and tiptoed passed Motti, but because I was rushed, I completely forgot about my dog. I knew if he saw me he would start barking. My body froze as our eyes caught. I prayed he would keep quiet.

"Shhhhhh, Motti, please don't bark. I beg you," I whispered.

Acting as if he had understood me, he plopped down without making a sound.

I breathed a sigh of relief.

I carefully opened the sliding door, taking my final step out into the warm summer breeze.

I felt like I'd won an award of a lifetime. I let out a quiet quick laugh, silently congratulating myself for getting out of the house.

But now it was back to work.

I ran to the front yard where the Acura was parked. My heart raced as I unlocked the shiny gold SUV Acura and shot myself into the cold leather driver's seat. I inserted the key into the ignition. I hesitated, worrying about the sound it would make as I was about to turn the key. But I had already gone too far to quit. I wasn't about to let my plan fail after going through all that playground sliding down stairs shit. Hell no.

I quickly turned the key, leading the car to awaken. I drove up the hill out of earshot from my house and parked next to the nearest curve.

I jumped out with the engine still running. As I sprinted back toward my house, I imagined myself getting caught by my parents. A clear picture of my dad with the "cinto" (whipping belt) in his hand getting ready for chaos formed in my mind. I knew then it was definitely a vision from God. I started to think this wasn't a good idea.

"Really? Out of all things, the cinto?" I asked God, looking up into the dark summer sky. "I hate the cinto."

I thought about all the whippings my dad had given me—each syllable he spoke interrupted by the burning sting. "I" BAM "told" BAM "you" BAM. The sound of his belt ricocheting across my body echoed in my head. It gave me a chill thinking about the cinto once again coming to life.

"Shit! What the hell should I do? Should I stay or should I run? Man, fuck it, I'm going."

I snuck back into my house to turn off the shower water, signaling to my parents I was done. Once again I started to think about the consequences if I was caught. I took a big gulp as I thought about my dad's temper. If he caught me, I would need to reserve a room at the hospital. Picturing dad looming over me with his short banged, slicked-back hair, broad shoulders and angry face made me shiver. I thought about the last time he smacked me across the face, nearly making my head turn a full 360 like in the movie "The Exorcist." That was for a minor reason. I didn't want to imagine how it would be if it was severe.

I've got to pull myself together. I've got this.

As fast as I could, I once again slid down the stairs, tiptoed past my dog, hurried out the back door and ran up the little hill. Hearing the car engine was music to my ears. I was free.

Once in the car, I grabbed my phone and messaged Chupi, letting him know I was on my way. As I put the car in driving position, my conscience once again kicked in. It felt like there was a hundred pound weight on my foot, preventing me from lifting it onto the gas pedal. I had a horrible feeling something bad was going to happen if I left with the car. But I forced the thoughts out of my head and hit the acceleration.

I was nervous as I turned onto the freeway to make the twenty-minute drive to Chupi's place. I tried to calm myself by playing Christian music from my iPhone. I played the song "God is Merciful," telling myself that God was merciful enough to keep my parents asleep while I was away if I listened to His music.

By the time I made it to Chupi's place, it was nearly one-thirty in the morning. As I turned into the neighborhood of duplexes, I turned off my headlights to keep from being spotted. I parked next to a small playground in the middle of the neighborhood, messaged Chupi and waited. He didn't have a phone, just an iPod, so the only way to reach him was through text messages.

I messaged him several more times and kept waiting. Everything was quiet and soothing, I was sleepy and my eyes were wearing out. I was suddenly jarred awake by the sound of something slamming into the passenger window. I felt the goose bumps flow through my body. It was Chupi.

"Where the hell have you been!" he yelled while getting comfortable in the passenger's seat. Chupi was only about five feet four, but he had a big personality with blue braces to go with it. He wore his hair short, emphasizing his oversized forehead.

I explained the process I had to go through to escape. When I was done, he started laughing like I had told a joke of a lifetime.

"Pretty embarrassing process, huh?"

"Very," Chupi agreed, still laughing.

We sat in the car, soaking up the moment. I cut off the Christian music, scanned to the song "The Motto" by Drake, and cranked up the volume on my iPhone.

"Now she want a photo, you already know though, you only live once, that's the motto nigga YOLO," we sang.

"YOLO" was our excuse for doing stupid things because we believed that if "you only live once," you had to make your life crazy and fun.

"You want to go pick up some friends?" Chupi asked, interrupting the song.

It annoyed me to have to pick up more guys. Besides the fact that they lived fifteen minutes away, these people weren't really my friends. I only saw them when we were cruising at night.

"All right," I sighed. "But will they put up some money for gas cause that's pretty deep to go all the way to Everett, then back here to drop you and everyone."

"Yeah, nigga, we got you."

"All right. You better not be playing, bro, cause shit, I don't want to be ending up on some random road because of no gas left," I barked.

I returned to the freeway going north to Everett. After three stops at different apartments, we picked up the friends Chupi had already notified. I felt like I was a taxi driving Chupi and his friends around the city of Everett.

I was starting to regret my decision to leave the house. *Was this really worth it? I was exhausted and overall bored. I was risking all of this trouble for this?*

I thought back to the nights before and how they'd been so much more fun: picking up girls, egging houses of the people we didn't like, racing down the streets going more than a hundred miles per hour. That was why the gas was drained down by the time I was on my way home. But everyone always came through with gas money.

"Aye Nata. We should hit up some females so they can come cruising with us. What do you say?"

Chupi was finally talking my language. He knew female company was well appreciated by me every time we went cruising at night.

"Hell yeah is what I say," I replied. I felt my mood lifting. Maybe the night would turn out okay after all.

Chupi texted a girl he knew would be down to sneak out and we were on our way to get her.

It was almost two in the morning by the time we arrived at the cluster of Everett apartments where she lived. We sat waiting as Chupi tried to call and text her. The minutes passed with no sign of her. I started to feel the tension and anxiousness of the guys in the car.

"Where the hell is she, dawg?" Chupi's friend asked.

The minutes turned into what felt like hours going by. I could feel my blood boiling. We'd come here and were wasting time for no reason. I felt like going up to the chick's door and screaming for her to come out.

"Screw the girl!" Chupi's friend said finally, waking up the silence.

"Yeah, Nata. How about let's go to Mariner and mess around there? I heard it was haunted and that things happen during the night," Chupi added.

At this point, I didn't even care. All hope was lost for a fun night.

"Alright then, let's go chill there," I replied.

We made our way to Mariner High School, and parked behind the school in a dark alley. A few feet ahead of us was a chain-link fence.

"Hey! Let's climb over and see if we find any signs of ghost!" I suggested.

"Ha-ha, alright," Chupi replied.

We climbed over the fence to the inside of the campus field. As soon as we locked our eyes on the ten-foot-high portable building where the game tickets were sold, we knew we'd found our chill spot.

"Let's get up there so we can hang on the roof," Chupi's friend said.

It was tough but we managed to hoist each other to the top and then worked together to pull the last person onto the roof.

Once there, we all started telling scary stories, making up stuff that had happened to us in our past lives. We tried to scare each other into believing that the Mariner Campus was haunted.

"I'm going to take a leak. I'll be back," Chupi said.

One of Chupi's friends continued on with his story. I felt someone grab my arm and jumped.

"What the hell!" I yelled.

It was Chupi, playing a trick. Everybody laughed.

"That was a good one, huh bro!" Chupi said, laughing.

"Fuck you nigga!" I replied, joining the laughter.

All my regrets about the night went away. I felt the joy of being with Chupi and his friends, swapping stories and chilling in the late summer night. It had turned into a perfect escape.

Just then we heard sirens from a police car. Fear hit me in the back of my spine. Now I had much bigger problems to think about. If I got caught, not only would I end up in the hospital from my dad's beatings, but life as I knew it would be over. The vision God gave me earlier that night flashed through my mind, but it was too late to make any changes. Why hadn't I listened to my instincts and God? I already had a first offense with the law for stealing at the mall. My mom had warned me it was the first and last time she would get me out.

I needed to figure out what to do. But with so much pressure in my head, it was nearly impossible to plan anything.

"Pigs down the field! Let's get out of here!" Chupi yelled.

We all jumped off the roof onto the hard cement. No one seemed be thinking about the pain. It was as if we were all used to jumping off roofs. We sprinted back to the car and I quickly opened the doors to let everybody in. Looking in my rearview mirror, I saw two police officers running toward us, their flashlights beaming.

"Get out of the car now!" one of the cops yelled.

There was an explosion of panicked voices around me. But I couldn't hear a sound. I froze, trying to figure out what to do.

"Nata! We got to get out of here!" Chupi yelled, shaking me.

I snapped back to my senses. He was right. I had to get the hell out of there and fast because there was no way I was going to spend the night at juvenile hall.

"Where the hell do I go!?" I demanded.

"Go to my pad! Hurry, bro! We can't get caught. I have weed in my backpack," Chupi's friend urged.

Weed? In my car? How could this be happening?

"Shit!" I yelled.

I floored the accelerator, checking the rearview mirror every three seconds to see if there was any sign of cops. I almost crashed into a car in front of me. I felt my body harden like steel as I tightened my grip on the steering wheel. I held on as hard as I could, closing in on Chupi's friend's apartment. I could hear the sirens from the other side of the block. Knowing the cops were looking for us, I pulled into the dark shadows of the apartment complex parking lot. I parked with all the other cars, hoping mine would blend in and make it difficult for the cops to find. We all ran into Chupi's friend's apartment, trying to catch our breath. I threw myself onto the living room couch, trying to keep myself from puking from all the heavy breathing.

"You are one crazy motherfucker for driving away from the cops bro!" Chupi's friend laughed, pointing at me.

"Aye, I had to do what I had to do to not get caught," I returned, still catching my breath. "I've been through trouble already with the law and wasn't going to have some again."

For a few minutes, the only sounds were heavy breathing. My head pulsed with the beat of my heart as I thought about our close call. I felt the heaviness of my eyelids. Then everything went black.

I woke up with a start. I looked around, confused. Nothing looked familiar. That's when it hit me: I wasn't home yet.

"Shit!"

I reached over to Chupi, who was sleeping on the floor, and began shaking him.

"Chupi, what time is it, man? I think I overslept!"

Chupi groaned. He was too knocked out. I wasn't going to waste my time trying to wake him up.

Panic shot through me as I frantically struggled to take out my phone from my jeans so I could check the time.

That's when I saw that I had ten missed calls and one text message.

My stomach was in knots. I wanted to throw up. I didn't want to listen to the voice messages and didn't want to look at the text message, fearing it would be my dad.

This was a lot more terrifying than when the cops were chasing me. If it was my dad, I knew my life was over.

I quickly glanced at my phone clock. It read five a.m. My mind raced with thoughts and questions.

It's impossible for dad to wake up for work this early. Dad usually wakes up at six-thirty. But who else could it be?

I took a deep breath, praying for it to be anyone else but him. My palms grew slick with sweat. I forced my eyes to look at the text. I immediately recognized his number.

I knew some deep can of whoop ass Bruce Lee shit was waiting for me at home.

"I want you here now," his message read.

I felt my heart pumping, my mind racing, my body trembling. It was like I'd had the weight of the world dropped on my shoulders. I wanted to be anyone else. I wanted any other person's life but mine.

"Chupi," I whispered, shaking him again. "I gotta go. My dad knows."

Chupi groaned again, rolled over and opened his eyes. I could tell my words registered. But he wasn't awake enough to fully understand the mess I was in.

"Okay, then," he said, rubbing his eyes. "I'm sorry, man. Hope you ain't in too much heat."

A Note from Nata

I'm now seventeen years old. Luckily, I got home safe that morning and, because my cousin had recently moved in with us and was there, I didn't get the beating I was expecting. Thank God. Since then, I've taken the motto "YOLO" to a different level. That was the last night I took the car out without my parents' permission. I learned to be more responsible and waited until I got my driver's license to drive; I didn't want to jeopardize my parents' trust. I started to acknowledge more about my life and knew I wanted to be successful. I now try to listen more to my instincts and, above all, God. I have my life together and I'm planning on graduating from Scriber Lake High School and going to college. I have my grades up and am trying to make much less stupid decisions in life. I've learned that life isn't about making crazy, stupid, unreasonable decisions all the time. It's really about making changes and decisions that will affect your life forever in a positive way. That's what "YOLO" is all about.

REPLACED

TATTIYANNA FERNANDEZ

Here I stand in a room that I should recognize, but it's completely different. It's not my room. It's not the room that I painted, not the room I slept in just last week. I knew things were going to be different, and I knew I would have to share a room with the baby if it was a girl, which it was. But I didn't know they were going to completely change my room.

My light pink-colored walls, my twin-sized bed, my heart-patterned bed spread, my paintings and posters are all gone. The chandelier my dad put in especially for me, my clothes, my dresser…everything is gone. Just like that. It looks like a full on nursery. Baby clothes, baby toys and a crib. The walls are now purple with lady bugs and butterflies.

Where is all my stuff? Where's my bed? Where's all my art? Where do they expect me to sleep. With the dog? All these thoughts that are screaming and chanting in my head want to come out, but I won't let them. I know it's over. It's the day I know my dad is going to forget all about me.

I feel betrayed. Just weeks before, my step-mom and I had a conversation on the phone.

"Hey, are you busy? I know you're getting ready to go camping with Payton but I wanted to ask you something," she said, all chipper-sounding, like usual.

"Alright, what's up?" I replied. I was worried because whenever she started a conversation like that, it was something bad.

"Well, if the baby is a girl, would it be okay if you guys shared a room? Being it's already girly and stuff?" she asked.

I breathed a sigh of relief.

"Yeah, I'd be okay with that, as long as she doesn't cry too much! Ha-

ha," I said, tying to joke around.

"Well, she wouldn't sleep there for a few months," she said.

"Oh, well, yeah, if it's a girl I'm totally fine with sharing my room," I said again, happy she had asked me first.

I had been completely fine with sharing my room with her. But when I see my changed room and all my stuff gone, it feels like there is a big rubber ball stuck in my throat. I want to cry, but I can't. Everything is blurry. I am looking at the new lady bug mini-ceiling fan through tears.

When I was growing up, my dad was in an immigration prison and my mom would take me to see him. We didn't go that often, but I can remember every single visit. I would talk to him through a glass window that was so scratched up I could barely see him, and a smelly pay phone thing that I was always scared to touch with my bare hands. We never stayed long and the conversations were always the same.

"How's it going, baby?" he would ask me.

"Fine, how about you, dad?" I would respond. I was always really shy so it was weird talking to him. He looked so different. He had always been such a put-together Armenian man. He always had the nicest shoes and suits and smelled so good. But behind glass he looked sloppy, like a caveman.

Mom would always save me from the awkward situation and get on the phone. Sometimes, if I was in a good mood, I would talk his ear off until we had to leave. It was always about my new school or my best friend.

"I met a new girl, her name is Payton and her birthday is two days after mine," I told him one day.

"Really, is she in your class?" he answered with a smile on his face.

I was so happy, I felt loved and appreciated. The look in his eyes told me I was the best part of his life.

"Yeah, we have Mr. Babb. She's my new best friend. She's short like me but she has blonde hair and blue eyes. And her mom and auntie are twins. Isn't that so cool?" I was so excited about my story that my heart raced.

"That's awesome, honey. I'm glad you like school," he said with a hint of sadness in his voice.

A few minutes later, we said our goodbyes. I could see the sadness in his eyes. This was always the hardest part. He would always tell me how special I was to him. I never wanted to leave; I wanted to stay there forever looking at him through that scratchy glass that blocked me from hugging him.

I knew that he really cared and loved me, and every year on my birthday until my sister was born, he would throw surprise birthday parties for me. I always had the best birthdays. Even when he was locked up, I felt his presence. But today, standing in the room that was once mine, I know that I will never see that look of 'I love you' anymore unless he is looking at my newborn little sister. I feel forgotten. My get-away place, my safe room, is gone with a blink of an eye.

I try to hold on to the old memories, to the times when everything was better. I wish I could be that little girl again, talking through the scratched-up glass, seeing that my father loves me. My stomach tightens into a knot and I want to puke all over the new purple walls. The warm touch of my dad's hands on my bare shoulders brings me back to reality, causing me to jump a little.

"Hey, kid," he says.

"Hey, dad, what's up?" I reply, trying to hold back the tears that are filling my eyes.

"You like your sister's room?"

He asks this like it's something I should be excited about.

I want to say, "No, dad. I hate it. I hate everything about it. I hate you. I hate your new wife and I'm not a part of this family and never will be. This is my room and I want all my stuff back in here by next week. I wish I never had a sister in the first place. And this is NOT her room, it's M I N E."

But instead all I say is, "Ehh, it's alright, but where did all my stuff go?"

"Well, ah, all your clothes are in a bag in the garage and your bed is at your grandma's house along with all your other stuff," he says. I can hear the hesitation in his voice. He avoids any eye contact with me, like he knows he is in the wrong.

I want to burst into tears, but I don't want to make a fool of myself. So I walk out, kind of bumping him. I need a place to be alone, a place to cry. I head to the bathroom and lay in the tub—fully dressed—for a half an hour, just thinking and crying the whole time. *Why am I not a good enough daughter for him to love me for who I am? Why would he just take all my stuff and pack it away like I had passed away or went off to college? I am only ten years old and already he has forgotten my existence?*

Ever since he'd been out of immigration prison, my dad was always telling me the things I did wrong. He wanted me to be in sports and all kinds of out-of-school activities, but I had been doing my own thing for so long that him telling me his plans for me felt out of place. None of it was going to happen. I had always had a smart mouth, too, and he hated it.

I know his new daughter will do anything he wants her to do and he will love it. He will love the fact that she is nothing like me.

When I finish crying, I leave the bathroom and put my school bag in the hall closet. Now I have nowhere else to put my stuff. The closet is the only place I can sort of call my own.

"Hey, dad!" I yell.

"Yes?" he yells back while walking up the stairs.

I decide to meet him at the top of the stairs to continue the conversation.

"Where am I going to sleep now?" I ask, trying not to cry again.

"Well, ah, you can sleep in your brother's room on the, ah, floor. Or maybe, if you want, on the couch. But that's where the dog sleeps, so I don't know if you want to do that. It's up to you," he tells me.

At that point I'm too angry to speak. *The dog has a place, but I don't?* I am so hurt and broken. I can't believe my own father could do something this horrible to me.

I end up on the couch with the dog, Ace, an English Mastiff that is bigger than me. I try to get comfortable with the snoring dog on top of me. Eventually, when my eyes can't cry any longer, I fall asleep, squished and heartbroken.

A Note from Tatti

I am now sixteen years old. I recently started talking to my dad again. Things have been getting better between us but I still need to get over my resentment towards him and my little sister. I wish to have a better relationship with my dad's side of the family. I plan to graduate on time next year. I am currently happy with the way things are going because I know my future is bright. I have been focusing mainly on school and my relationship with my boyfriend and friends. My passion is drawing and I want to become a tattoo artist and a phlebotomist (someone who draws blood).

WHAT SHE SHOULD HAVE SAID

MAGGIE HIGGINS

Every day mom and I fight. She screams, I scream, and it's all just madness.

Today was like any other day. It was terrible. Of course, I skipped most of my classes and just moped around. When I got home from school, I thought about all the negative things from the day and let it out on my skin with a razor blade. Mom knows I do this, and doesn't like it. But I don't care. I do what I want to my skin.

Mom's home now. I can tell because the door always slams behind her. She walks up the stairs heavily and I can hear her clackers on the hardwood floors. Click, clack, every step she takes, click clack, as her heels hit the floor. I cringe at this sound. It's like her anger is piercing into the floor with her heels that look like they could cut your head off. At this point, I would quite enjoy my head being cut off.

I stop cutting and sit with the razor blade in one hand and a slit wrist on the other arm, one hand resting on each knee. I listen to mom's footsteps to see where she is so I know when she will come downstairs to start the battling. I hear her heavy footsteps coming down the stairs, and my heart starts to race. I hear her heels again on the floor when she reaches the hallway because the hall is bare, with no carpet because of the floods. One flood was from the washer overflowing, and the other two were from the rain. My family tends to never finish projects, so our house is one big unfinished project.

She gets closer with every step, until finally, I see the side of her tall, slightly chunky figure in the doorway. Her makeup-free face is oily as it always is at the end of the day, and her deep-red lipstick has faded. I feel every muscle in my body tense up. But she continues walking to the end of the hall to the laundry room. I breathe out, like a partial sigh of relief. I didn't even realize I was holding my breath. I stay still and don't move at all, not knowing what her next move will be. I can smell her dense old-lady perfume lingering at my door. She opens the dryer door and begins pulling out the clean clothes; I hear zippers clanking against the opening of the dryer. The smell of the dryer sheets gives me some comfort. All I want is for her to help me, to support me and be sensitive to my needs. But I never get that from her.

I slowly slide the blade under my thigh, grab my sketchbook and act like I'm drawing. I hear mom take a deep breath. I know what this means.

"You forgot to clean the litter box again!" she yells as though I'm not just in the other room. Her dull, angry voice makes me flinch. "And you didn't give the cats more food. Did you do your other chores?"

"No," I answer quietly.

"What?" she yells.

"No, I didn't. I forgot," I say a little louder.

"How could you forget? I asked you to do two things. Two. And you forget. Let me guess. You haven't done your homework either," she says before walking back upstairs. She doesn't even look in my room when she walks past, which is kind of a relief. I throw my sketchbook on top of my bag, slide the razor blade back out from under my leg, and go back to slicing my wrist open—slowly dragging the blade horizontally across my skin and digging it in deep to get a sufficient amount of blood draining. I don't know why I do this to myself, and I don't know why I even started, but ever since the first time mom found out I cut, she just gets more and more angry.

I can hear her coming back down the stairs. This time I don't panic.

Nothing can stop me from hurting myself like this. Right now, in this moment, I don't care. I don't care if mom walks in. I don't care if I stain the carpet with my blood. I don't care if these wounds I am creating for the sadness I feel in this one moment in my life leaves scars forever. I want to stop feeling like I have to physically hurt myself for my emotional pain, but I can't seem to control it.

I hear her footsteps stop at my doorway, and I can feel her presence. Keeping my head down, I see her out of the corner of my right eye. I see her thin, brown, shoulder-length hair as she looks down at me. I'm sitting crisscross applesauce on the soft brown sugar-colored carpet in front of my mirror, my usual spot for cutting. I know she sees the blood slowly leaving my body because my arm is wrist-up, resting on my knee. I don't dare look at up at her. I know exactly what look is on her face. Tears will just barely pool up in the inner corner of her hazel eyes.

I look up, but only with my eyes. Through my hair I see her clenched fists, and hear a heavy, angry-sounding sigh. She starts to yell. I can't make out what she's yelling, though. All I hear is her dull, angry voice screaming. I keep my head down. I feel an intense fear rushing deep inside me and can feel her staring down at me, her pointy heels slightly sinking into the carpet. I feel her anger shooting through her eyes, penetrating me like sharp needles.

I sit shaking, scared, on the verge of terrified, not knowing what her next move will be. It's like a horror movie, where you hear the background music getting more and more intense, and you know the boogey monster is going to jump out. I can smell a hint of salt from my fear-sweat, lightly pooling on my back. She stops screaming. Then I see her foot start to move. Time freezes for a moment because of the fear of not knowing what's coming next. I snap back to real time and shock hits me. My brain cannot register what it's from. All I can feel is myself shaking. I start moving towards the door, but I'm not walking. I feel pressure on the middle of my upper arm. I then realize it's my mother's hand, her grip getting tighter.

I let out a scream, deep from my lungs. I start to tug back as she pulls me closer to the door. I don't know where she is taking me. All I can think is that I can't let her take me out of my room. But I am defeated. She has managed to drag me into the hallway. I pull harder and start to flail my feet so that she loses her grip, and my arm drops to the floor. I quickly pull it into me. She bends down, closer to me, trying to retrieve my arm. I curl up into somewhat of a ball, slightly up on my knees, trying to be cautious of the wood strip of nails on the edges of the hallway that hold the carpet down. I cradle my arm close to my chest. She's on her knees now, hovering over me. She starts to pick and pull and prod, trying to get my arm back. I hold it tight to my chest. She keeps fighting, trying to get it, and I get more on my knees so my chest is facing the ground and my head is on the floor.

She finally grabs my arm again. Her grip is tight around my wrist, opposite of the one I cut. I try to pull it back, but she pulls harder, and I start sliding down the hall.

My mother continues to pull me down the short hallway. There are no sounds, no talking. *Why isn't she saying anything?* The sound of her heavy breathing makes me even more nervous. She should be yelling, screaming, but it's like her anger is just built up inside. I am afraid that all that built up anger will be released with such power that she will lose control. The not knowing is what scares me—the unpredictable future, the fear of being hurt by someone other than myself. I continue to try to pull my arm back, but it just causes pain in my wrist like my hand is being pulled out of its socket. My body rotates to the right as she pulls me into the bathroom. The tile isn't even with the hallway floor and my hip hurts as it runs over the edge.

My mom continues dragging me, and the thin purple bath rug starts to roll up as my body is pulled across it. She finally lets go of my wrist, My elbow goes straight into my gut because I didn't realize I was still pulling my arm back.

The natural blue- and green-colored tile is hard and cold and I feel it on my thigh through my sweatpants. The bathroom is dirty. It always is. There is this dust that covers the bathroom and is impossible to get rid of. You can't see it, but it's there. You can feel it on your bare feet when you walk in with no socks.

My mother opens the medicine cabinet that is above the pedestal sink to the left of me. She steps over me and starts going through the dresser that is a replacement for a counter and cabinets in my bathroom. She opens one drawer, slams it closed, opens another, slams that one, opens a third. I hear her moving things around in the drawer, searching for something—what, I'm not sure. She then walks back over to me, steps over my legs again and sits on the closed toilet seat. I keep my head down, hair covering my eyes, and stare at the dusty, cold tile. I haven't moved one bit since she dragged me in here.

"Give me your arm," she says. I refuse and don't move.

She grabs it and my body jerks because that is the arm I was leaning on. I feel a stinging, burning pain on my cuts. I flinch and tug my arm, but she has a strong grasp on my hand. I look up and see that she is not pouring, but dumping alcohol on my wrist.

"Stop!" I yell, because it really hurts.

"This shouldn't hurt if you hurt yourself intentionally," she says. That shocks me. I know she's right, and my mind wanders, trying to make sense of it all. I hurt myself intentionally to heal the emotional pain, but I still feel the physical pain. I'm not numb, and it does hurt, yet I still do it. She continues to try to clean my wounds.

Finally she stops and sets the bottle on the sink. There is a puddle of alcohol on the floor slightly bubbling, just like it is doing on my skin. She wipes my arm with toilet paper to dry it, and that makes the sting worse. She then rubs Neosporin on my cuts. It's a soothing feeling compared to the awful sting of the alcohol. Mom stands up, steps over me, rounds the slight corner and walks out the bathroom door. She just leaves me sitting on the floor, feeling this terrible pain—both inside and out.

I don't know what to think. I am stunned. Time stops as I try to register what just happened. It was so abrupt, but my mind is blank, and I can only feel the sting that is starting to calm down on my wrist. I sit here, not moving.

I look at the alcohol bottle sitting on the sink and the puddle that has spilled on the floor. I look at the Neosporin tube resting on the toilet seat. I take in a deep breath. A tear starts to roll down my face, and I feel it fall on my knee. I curl up in a ball on the cold bathroom floor and just lay there crying.

A Note from Maggie

Each day I grow stronger trying to conquer my depression and battle the urges to cut. I have learned to speak out when I am struggling and to get help from my dad, a friend, my counselor, or my amazing girlfriend. My relationship with my mom is still a struggle, but she has not hurt me for two years. My dad is a really big support person in my life and I can turn to him for anything. As he learned in AA and has taught me, I take it one day at a time. My grades have gotten so much better and I attend all of my classes. Last year I went to Costa Rica with a group from my school and raised all of the money myself. In Costa Rica I really learned to appreciate what I have. When we visited a tribe I gave a little girl my hat. It warmed my heart to see how happy it made her, and how proud she was to wear it. I'm involved in Roller Derby, and skating is my biggest passion. Being in derby has helped develop me as an athlete and also as a person. It has helped teach me to be a leader in my community, and really put my best effort into everything I do.

CRUSH

SUMMER COOPER

You've got no chance! I tell myself as I dreamingly watch him walk into our third period class.

Ever since leaving Mountlake Terrace High School, I question everyone's motives, including my own. The last boy I fell in love with broke my heart and beat it with a hammer. He was super nice to everyone except for me. By the end, he would hold the door for one person then slam it in my face.

When I arrived at Scriber that first day, I saw a lot of guys. But I was convinced that nobody could ever compare to the guy at my other school—until I saw him. He has short brown hair that ends right above his eyebrows. His hair is straight but curls at the end and is covered with a red baseball hat. He wears a red jacket that goes to his knees. He is tall but not overwhelmingly tall. He has one of the most defined jaws I've ever seen.

Man, he's so cool, I think to myself. *But do you honestly think that if he could have all these perfect dolls that he would choose you?*

Every day I wait for him to enter the room. When he does, my breathing hitches and my throat becomes dry. I feel that if I move I will look like an idiot.

I'm sitting in class but I feel like I am on a reality TV show and if I make a mistake my life will be over. I can't let him know I like him, so I examine the room. It looks like every other classroom I've seen. There are bright lights, tables and a Jimi Hendrix poster by the door. I am running out of things to stare at. It smells like fresh printing paper so I try to concentrate on that but I can't; the urge to look at him is overpowering my ability to think. I turn my head swiftly and there he is, sitting at the table next to me.

He has eyes that change color every time you look at them. I think it's his smile that really stands out to me, though. There is also something about his laugh that intrigues me. It's deep, but cute in a way. He is really expressive and loud so his voice carries; because of that I can always tell when he is around. He is always talking in slang. I love the way that even when he is loud, there's a calming persona to him. You wouldn't think someone like him would know how to be respectful. But he is respectful from what I have seen.

I know I should stop staring, but I can't; it's like a magnetic force.

And just like that, he looks up at me. My heart starts beating rapidly and my hands start to sweat. *I am not good enough for him. He is perfect. I can't ever let him find out,* I say to myself like I'm talking to my best friend.

Class begins and I am truly interested in what the teacher is saying. But that magnetic force just won't stop distracting me.

The incident that happened two years earlier at Terrace flashes in my head like a show on reruns; the terrible ending playing over and over in my mind. I cringe as I think about the worst friend I have ever had. Shelly stood about 4'9 with dark skin and dark hair. Her short hair was always in a ponytail and she always wore all pink. I remember her walking up to me with a smirk on her face. I knew I wasn't going to like what she had to say to me. Her voice sent chills down my spine. It wasn't so much what she said—it was how she said it with her intimidating voice.

"Why do you bother with someone who will never care about you?" she asked.

I saw that coming but I didn't understand how she could be such a hypocrite, because the guy she liked didn't like her either.

Her words filled me with hurt and sadness.

"You're such a bitch," I whispered, just loud enough for her to hear. What irked me the most was how conceited she was. If I turned out like her I would have to hate myself. Fortunately, no one ever complimented me.

"Wow, great comeback. At least the guy I like I'm sort of friends with," she replied in a taunting manner.

I honestly didn't know how she thought that. She had never even talked to him outside of school.

When she noticed I wasn't going to say anything, she piped up again. "You basically stalk him."

I shot her a dirty look. I liked him a lot and I would stare at him because I thought he was attractive, but that's not stalking. Everyone stares at someone they like; it's not a crime. I never followed him around or took secret pictures. I never did anything that could even suggest I was stalking him.

Later that day I noticed his mood toward me had changed. He wouldn't go anywhere I was. If he saw me he would run the other way. Her words replayed in my head like a song on repeat, a song I didn't like. *You basically stalk him.*

It finally hit me what had happened; she had told him. I couldn't believe she could stoop that low. She knew how much he meant to me. Hatred burned through my chest like fire.

"Are any of you guys paying attention?" our irritated teacher yells.

I look over at him and he is sitting quietly with his eyes locked intently on the teacher, just like everyone else. "Okay, get out a piece of paper. We're doing a writing exercise," she says.

He gets up to get a piece of paper from the front of the room. On his way, he stops.

"Is that the new iPod Touch?" he asks.

Even though it is in my hands, it doesn't register that he is talking to me. It doesn't seem possible. Would someone that popular talk to me? Then it finally hits me that he is. My heart beat increases and I get nervous. I don't just get nervous, I get NERVOUS. My mind starts racing a thousand miles an hour and my hands begin to sweat. I don't even know what to do with them.

Do I put them on the desk or do I put them in my lap? I wonder. I want to speak, but it is like there is a wire in my brain missing that makes that impossible. I muster all the confidence I can find within my non-confident self.

"Yes!" I squeal.

I say it so quietly that I don't think he hears me. Regret overcomes me. I feel terrible. I had the opportunity to talk to him and I screwed it up. What if God doesn't give me another chance to talk to him? Will I forever remain just another person in his class?

"IPod touches are so cool. No one really uses MP3 players anymore," he adds.

Regret is replaced with complete bliss. I have never felt so happy in my life. As he walks back to his desk I can't stop smiling. I swear my face feels at least a shade of pink, if not red. I slowly put my head down, trying to hide it. Honestly, at this point in my life, no one can take me off cloud nine. I am beyond ecstatic.

Crazy thoughts begin to take over. *Does he know? Do his friends know? Am I making things too obvious? Does he think I am a stalker, too? What does he see when he sees me?*

All these questions consume me. This guy is perfect. I am not talking about Hollywood-movie perfect, I am talking about real-life perfect. He is popular, yet he's a really nice guy. His eyes shine like diamonds. His teeth aren't pearly white or perfectly straight, but that's what makes his smile perfect to me. In my eyes, imperfection is sometimes imperfectly perfect.

Looking back on the past and experiencing the present, I know that in order to make sure that nothing tragic happens with this guy, I have to keep this all to myself. I know that if I had not told my former friend that I liked the guy at my previous school, he and I could have at least been friends. *If I am the only one who knows, nothing can go wrong.*

The bell finally rings. As the class exits, I take one final look and thank God we have the same lunch.

❦

A Note from Summer

I'm an eighteen year-old Christian Leo with a dysfunctional family. I was born in Washington State and I have never left. Not much has changed regarding the boy in my story.

I'm still trying to find the courage to speak to him; I will never know if I might gain a friend if I don't try. The friend that betrayed me is no longer in my life.

On a positive note, for the first time in my life I am doing what I need to do, and I have become a successful student at Scriber Lake. I have performed four times in front of the school this year: twice with a program called 'Rain City Rock Camp for Girls' where we formed a band with other female students. I was the lead singer and songwriter. I also performed two songs for the school's talent show, 'Believe' and 'All around the World' by Justin Bieber. My biggest inspirations are my family, my best friend, Jazmine, her sister Shaylene, Rob Thomas, Taylor Swift, Justin Bieber, Pattie Mallette and God. I plan to graduate next year and my dream is to have a career in singing and songwriting. I hope my story has affected you in a positive way, along with all the other stories in this book.

MY FIRST DATE

DEANNA TITTLE

I could feel my feet getting numb, the sweat dripping from my body. I couldn't move. It was almost like I was paralyzed. My vision started going fuzzy, but I could still see Jeremiah sitting on the other side of his bed loading the pipe. He didn't even notice there was something wrong with me. All he cared about was smoking the rest of the shit and getting high.

❧

I was only twelve when I first met Jeremiah. He was tall and had pale skin, crystal blue eyes and soft brown hair. You could smell the Versace and spice coming off him from miles away. He was fifteen and everything about him attracted me.

We were at Jake's house, where I had been living for about a year. I felt more welcome there because no one ever yelled at me or tried to blame all their problems on me like they did at home. We would always hang out in Jake's garage and party. The garage smelled of stale beer, cigars and puke. There were hundreds of empty bottles on the shelves, garbage bags piled on top of each other, and cigarette butts scattered across the floor. In the middle there was a circle of broken chairs with a beer pong table on the side. As usual, we'd been smoking and drinking all day. It wasn't until I got drunk that I noticed Jeremiah and talked to him. After that night we were inseparable.

The day he asked me out we had already been hanging out for about two years. We had just woken up from a long night of partying.

"Babe, let's have a day of our own today. I'll take you out." He grinned as he tucked my hair behind my ear.

My heart started tingling. I was so overpowered by happiness. "Where are we going?" I asked.

Maybe he's going to take me out to an expensive dinner and plan the night to make me feel special, I thought. My mind was going on about all the different things we could do. I just wanted him to spend his money on me and take me somewhere nice.

"We are going to take a trip down to Fremont," he replied. My eyes sparkled and I smiled.

"What's in Fremont?" I asked with hope. I didn't know anything about Fremont.

"It's a surprise. You'll see," he said.

He wasn't licensed yet, so we called up one of his friends to get a ride. When we finally got to Fremont we walked up to a group of four guys in the parking lot of a rundown building. They spoke Spanish and their clothes were all torn up and splattered with paint. They looked like construction workers.

Why are we meeting up with these people? I thought to myself.

They took Jeremiah around the corner and I saw him pull out a stack of money and get handed a small bag. I knew then that he had just bought an 8ball of crack. I had seen him buy it before and I had been smoking it for six months by then. We weren't really on a date, we were just going to get our daily dose.

We walked around Fremont for at least two hours after that. The whole time we walked I was forcing back the tears. I didn't want to be there. I just wanted to go home and get high and forget the disappointment. He finally asked me if I wanted to leave.

"Yes!" I yelled.

We called our ride and got picked up to go back to Mountlake Terrace.

We made it to his house around 7 pm and headed for his bedroom. He lived in the smallest two-bedroom house with his sister, Juliet, and his mom, Viola. His sister's bedroom door was wide open. She was like a sister to me.

"Hi girl, want to smoke a cigarette with me?" she asked.

"I'd love to."

She looked exactly like Jeremiah: brown hair with piercing blue eyes and an olive skin tone. I followed her outside. While we smoked, Jeremiah went into his bedroom to get a hit ready for me.

I finished the cigarette and headed to his room. When I walked in, I could tell he had hit the pipe already. He was on his small twin bed breathing extremely hard. I started getting this feeling like there were a whole bunch of butterflies swarming around in my stomach. I would always get that feeling right before I got high. It was an adrenaline rush just knowing I was going to leave this world and go into my own imagination dream.

He cooled down the pipe with a wet sock and I could hear the sizzling of the water in the sock hitting the pipe. Then he loaded me a hit. I reached over to grab the pipe and took in that first hit. The taste of the stale, cold smoke entered my body, Panic and anxiety ran through my veins. The smoke tasted like I had just gone to the dentist and got my teeth cleaned, like chemicals. My brain was booming against my skulls as I slowly got up and closed the blinds. I heard someone slam the front door and my heart dropped.

"Who is that?" I asked, panicking,

"Oh, babe, don't worry. It's just my mommy," he replied.

His mom never cared what we were doing. All she cared and worried about were her own problems.

He just kept on loading the pipe with more hits. The 8ball we had gotten was almost gone. On my last hit I fell back on the bed. I could feel pressure on my body like someone was pushing on me. The heat that took over made me sweat so much it looked like I had just stepped out of a shower. My body suddenly went stiff and everything around me got distorted. I watched Jeremiah load himself another hit. He didn't take one glance at me. I felt abandoned at the worst possible time. I started to shake and felt tingly. Then I heard a quiet voice coming from the door; I thought I was dreaming it.

"Jeremiah, what the hell is going on? What is wrong with her?" asked Jeremiah's mom in the sweetest pissed-off voice.

"Nothing, Mom. She's fine," he replied.

"Look at her. She is NOT fine," I heard her say as she walked toward me.

The next thing I knew, my face was cold and my hands were wet. My eyes slowly opened and there was Jeremiah's mom right above me with an ice-cold rag and a bucket of cold water. She had taken me into the bathroom. The lights were so bright and my eyes so heavy that I let them drop closed. I could feel the acid in my stomach. I had no energy, no motivation to even move my feet. All I could think about was taking another hit to get rid of my dope sick.

I hung my head over the toilet, then slowly forced myself up. As I got up and looked in the mirror, my heart broke at what stared back at me: hollow eyes, sunken cheeks. I looked so unhealthy.

How could I ever let myself get this way?

A Note from Deanna

There are two roads you can go by, but in the long run/There's still time to change the road you're on.—"Stairway to Heaven," Led Zeppelin

I left Jeremiah's house the next day without once turning back because I realized I was following in the footsteps of my parents. They had been addicts for seven years of my life. I'm sixteen now and I've been clean for two years. My parents got a divorce and my mom and I helped each other get clean. If you struggle with addiction, there's always a way out if you have the proper support. I enrolled in online school so I could be at home, away from the temptation to use again. In those two years I completely changed my group of friends, and when I went back to school, I enrolled at Scriber. I'm still struggling, but my mom and I support each other. My goals are to graduate from Scriber and head to a four-year university.

HE WAS MY HERO

ISABEL CORDOVA

It's been eight months since my dad and I have talked to each other. I am ready to confront him, and tell him that I am sorry and ask him to forgive me.

I am sitting at our dark wooden kitchen table with my mom, my boyfriend and his parents, waiting for my dad's arrival. I'm excited, but at the same time scared that he is going to try to hit me again—this time in front of my boyfriend. While I wait I think about running and forgetting about it all. I also want to just scream at him and ask, "Why? And how could you hit your own daughter the way you did that night?"

But I decide to be patient and wait for him to get home. These two hours are the longest I've ever waited for someone. While we wait, we eat pepperoni and sausage pizza from Domino's. We're laughing and talking as usual; things are always light and easy when it's just us.

The night that everything changed I had spent the day hanging out with my boyfriend and some friends. I had arrived home late and my dad wasn't home yet, so I was relieved. My dad's bad temper and serious face scared me sometimes. Most of the time I was forced to confess to him where I was and who I was with.

It was about two o'clock in the morning when my dad burst in my room. I was half asleep in my bed, lying sideways, when the lights went on and I felt the cold air as he ripped my blanket off of me. I felt a stinging and burning as he whipped my thighs with the heavy, black leather belt he always carried. I opened my eyes in time to see him fling his arm behind his head to increase the force of the blow each time he hit me.

Was I having a nightmare? This couldn't be real. It had to be a bad dream. He couldn't be doing this. Is that you, Dad? It's me, Isabel. Do you know you are hurting me?

I felt the next blow of the belt, cutting into my legs. I heard myself scream from the pain and scrambled to sit up in my bed and pull my legs away from him.

"STOP IT DAD!" I begged, trying to push him away.

"Where the fuck were you today!?" I could smell alcohol and his black greasy hair. The evil, mean look on his face scared me.

"Hanging out with my friends," I cried.

Thank God the beating had stopped, but I knew the verbal assaults were about to start— which for me were more harsh and brutal than his physical abuse. My dad was the type of person who didn't care about whose feelings he hurt or about what others thought of his verbal or physical assaults.

"NO! Do you think I'm stupid? Stop fucking lying to me! A friend told me they saw you holding hands with a boy, coming out of some apartments! I'm telling you Isabel, I don't want any fucking slutty, skanky hoes living in my house!! So you better get the fuck out!" He looked at me as if I was disgusting and not worth anything.

I stayed frozen and didn't speak. There was no point in trying to defend myself. Even if I tried he wouldn't listen to me; he always had to be right. So I just decided to stay quiet and cry my pain away.

Then I heard squeaky footsteps running toward my room. I knew instantly they were my mom's. My dad slowly backed away from the bed and just stood there.

"What did you do to her?" my mom screamed. Her face looked like she was about to beat the crap out of my dad. But at the same time, she looked sad and worried about me. I knew she was angry that he had laid a hand on me while I was asleep and when he was extremely drunk.

She started hugging me. That's when my dad decided to get out of my room, almost tripping over my mattress.

"Where do you think you're fucking going? Look what you have done to your daughter! You son of a bitch!" My mom yelled, nearly spitting her words in anger.

It was strange to see my mom so mad and screaming. She was usually calm, never swearing in front of my brothers or sister. I was surprised and happy that she had finally stood up against my dad for herself and her family. It was kind of funny seeing a five-foot-tall, skinny, black-haired lady swearing and screaming at a five-foot-eight man who was trying to act tough and manly.

"Everything is going to be okay," Mom said to me in a gentle voice.

I was in tears, crying into my mom's shoulder, trying to talk. But words wouldn't come out. All I could do was try to wrap my mind around what had just happened. I couldn't believe my dad had come home drunk and hit me like that. Or that he had said such horrible things to me, his own daughter. *What kind of father insults his own daughter the way he did?*

"No! It's not!" I finally stammered. "I don't want to be near him! I'm done dealing with him!" I was crying so hard my nose was running and I could hardly breathe.

My mom lay down next to me, held me close and drifted off to sleep. I tried to go to sleep, too, because I was tired and had to go to school the next day. I also didn't want to wake my mom. I knew that comforting me was only part of the reason she had stayed with me that night. She also wanted to watch me and make sure I didn't do anything dumb, like run away.

The next day I called my auntie to come and get me out of school so that I could have time to pick up my bags before my dad came back from work. That morning I had told my mom that I wasn't coming back home, that day or ever. She agreed that I should stay at my boyfriend's house for a while. I think she realized that I wasn't safe at home, that close to a man like my dad. The only thing she wanted was for me to be safe and happy. And if that meant being far away from her, then she was okay with it.

I hear the front door open. My dad, who was once my hero, my everything—just like I thought I was to him—has finally arrived. The plan is for my boyfriend's parents to talk to him while I wait in my room for the right moment to come out. But I can't help myself; I am so excited to hear his voice when he walks through the door that I immediately run toward him for a hug. The only thought racing through my mind is how much I love and miss him and how sorry I am. It doesn't occur to me that he doesn't feel the same way until I feel him push me.

"No!" he barks at me with anger.

I fight back tears when he says that word. Everyone around me is quiet and watching. I am hurt and angry. *Shouldn't it be me being mad at you for beating me up and leaving me bruises all over my legs?* I want to scream at him. *Shouldn't it be me mad at you for doing so much to me and making me the person I am? Shouldn't it be me mad at you for screwing up my health and life?*

I want to run away from everything and everyone. Not only do I feel unwanted by my own dad, I also feel embarrassed and humiliated by his rejection towards me, especially in front of my boyfriend's parents. My dad doesn't have any respect for the fact that they are there, staring at us.

I'm still reeling from his push, but his next words are the final blow. "My daughter is dead to me! I don't have a daughter anymore." He looks at all of us while he yells the words.

I feel my body heating up and going stiff. I feel my tears falling nonstop on my cheeks. I hear a door slam. He is gone.

My mom gets up from the kitchen table and rushes to me, hugging me and trying to comfort me with her love.

"It's okay, honey," she says softly, stroking my hair. "You know your dad loves you. It's just that he's mad at the moment. He'll get over it. Besides, you have me. You know I'll support you, whatever your choices are in life. Te quiero mucho mija."

I know deep inside that nothing is okay; I just want to yell out, *How does he love me, mom? By hitting me and rejecting me? By pushing me away from his life? By talking to me like I am the worst person in life? NO! He doesn't love me! That's not a real father, especially a real man! Nothing is okay! I'm not okay, mom.*

But I can't say anything like this to her because I don't want to cause her more stress and pain that will only add to her health issues. She has horrible migraines and recently had an operation to remove pre-cancerous tumors.

I can't hurt her more than she is already hurting. So I swallow my feelings, look at her and say, "I love you too, Mom."

A Note from Isabel

At this moment I am sixteen years old and I've had to mature faster than I ever thought I would. Last year I was struggling to keep my health up and was using drugs and alcohol as an escape from my own problems. I also didn't care about school and wouldn't even attend an hour of class. Now I am passing all my classes, trying to graduate from Scriber Lake High School, which has helped me get on track. I'm planning on going to college and owning my own salon in the future. I have also said goodbye to drugs and alcohol forever. Attending church is my escape now. I'm still with my boyfriend; I've been living with him for more than eight months. I have not talked to my dad for more than a year. I'm still hoping to get his forgiveness, because he has mine. I'm still in touch with my mom and I see her every other day. I am grateful for who I have become and what I have, and I thank God for every day I make it through.

"One's dignity may be assaulted, vandalized and cruelly mocked, but it can never be taken away unless it is surrendered."—Michael J. Fox

LIAR

ETHAN ELLIOTT

I insert the razor into my stomach, pushing in deeper to start the letter "L."

Without emotion, I watch the blood drain out of my stomach into one of the three paper towels I had grabbed from our master kitchen.

I don't know what has set me off today. I know I'm angry with my parents for never being home, for never being there for me. I know I'm feeling alone and abandoned like I always do. Whenever I feel like I am going to explode, I turn to cutting and pills. Today, it's cutting.

I finish carving the letter "L" into my flesh. The letter is about an inch and a half high, like something out of a horror movie. And it's deep. The sting of my stomach makes me tighten my body, reducing the blood flow. This is a good thing because I can't get blood on my down-feather orange comforter. I can't let my parents find out.

My parents had called me a liar because I told them I was at a friend's house when I was actually at home playing video games. What they don't know is that I have been lying to them about my whole life. I want to tell them the truth. But how do you tell your parents that they aren't there for you? At least not in the way that matters.

I shift the bloody razor to the right of the "L" and slowly insert it. Making the "I" is quick, just a straight line. I sit on my bed, staring at my orange and yellow checked wall, and out my window to the blackberry bushes. Rage rushes through me, turning my clenched hands red like my blood.

My eyes scan my room, taking in my X-Box, my flat screen TV, my mini fridge. Everyone thinks I am so lucky to have so much stuff. All it reminds me of is how alone and out of place I feel.

I hate being an only child, coming home to this huge empty house every day. *Why do we need such a big house when no one but me is ever here?*

This is my parent's dream house and it had been custom-built just for us. It has a fancy chef kitchen that opens into a huge living room and dining room. It has a large media room and a guest bedroom. On the top floor is my parents' master suite, which has its own Jacuzzi tub and walk-in shower. The room even has a balcony. I swear it's as big as a small apartment. Then there's my room, complete with my own bathroom. When we were building this house, my parents asked me if I wanted a big room. I had said yes. I didn't know it would end up torturing me.

My parents work late every night, sometimes not getting home until 9 pm. They buy me everything I want: video games, clothes, music. And the only one I have to share it with is my cat, Spencer. He is the only loyal and caring organism in my life. He's here with me now, curled up on my bed, watching me cut. Today, though, his company isn't enough.

I start carving the next letter, "A." I don't want to do it, but I tell myself it has to be finished. I don't make it as deep as the other letters because I'm already in a lot of pain.

I think back to the conversation I had with my parents a few nights before. I had wanted to tell them how I needed them, how I felt like they were never there. But I couldn't get the words out. Instead I decided to talk about an easier subject.

"Mom, Dad, I am having a hard time feeling in place at school," I told them. "I have lots of friends, but I still feel different."

I wanted them to guide me, to help me deal with the problems I have. But Mom's answer was short and to the point as usual.

"Ethan, I want you to know that you are going to be fine. Life is confusing, but you will be fine. Just give it time."

It was just a simple line. The line she always used. Dad said nothing, and that was the end of the conversation. They both said goodnight and headed upstairs to their room.

Maybe Mom was right. Maybe everything would eventually be fine. But I'm not fine now. I need Mom and Dad to tell me what to do.

"R." I don't want to do it, but I have to finish. I just keep telling myself over and over that I am a liar and need to be punished. But really I don't feel like I have a choice. I have to lie. Because what parent wants to hear that they aren't there for their kid?

The "R" is hard. Why are there so many lines in R? I feel queasy and my right hand shakes as I cut the final lines, holding the paper towel in my left hand to catch the blood.

Finally finished, I pick up the razor that is lying on my stomach. I look down at my torn apart flesh. The blood had filled up my last paper towel and is running down my stomach. I quickly lean back against my wall, slightly tilted, so I can cup my hands and catch the blood, keeping it from getting on my blankets. *Why didn't I grab more paper towels?*

The pain is getting worse and I'm starting to panic a little. I look at my alarm clock. It reads 4 p.m. I have five more hours before my parents get home. Suddenly I'm really scared. What if I bleed out and die before they arrive home?

I could definitely use my parents. But after everything, I'm not about to ask them for help now.

I close my eyes, hoping to escape. As I drift off, I have one final thought: if I die and my parents find me, maybe they will finally know the truth.

A Note from Ethan

I have gotten better by anyone's standards. It took awhile, but my wounds from that day finally healed and I learned that cutting myself was a big mistake. I also discovered that my parents were never terrible parents and that they had made a good kid. I just had some problems. As I got older, I started opening up to my parents and discovered that they had been there for me all along. Over the past few years, I have learned to lean on others and to ASK for the help I need. I am now in counseling and therapy, which has helped me a lot. Today I'm an eighteen-year-old senior in high school. I've got some catching up to do, so I will be finishing high school next year. After graduating, I hope to get into either the medical field or robotics. I want the best for my family and friends. The upside of all of this is that I have found my real friends and the people that I can trust.

GONE

DESTINY ALLISON

My heart stopped when I heard my grandma speak the words. As if it wasn't bad enough hearing them the first time, they kept replaying in my head. "We went to your dad's house this morning. He's dead."

The rush of numbness washed over me and I felt my eyes fill with tears. I swallowed to try and hold them in. My grandma, who was sitting next to me on our brown leather couch, began to cry. My mom scooted towards me and wrapped her arms around me. That's when the tears began to flow. For a few moments I felt like a waterfall from the amount of water pouring from my eyes. I took a deep breath and sucked my tears back in.

I texted my best friend Maggie and told her I had bad news. She thought it was that my mom had lost the baby she was pregnant with. When I told her my dad had died, she and her girlfriend rushed to my house. As soon as they arrived, my first instinct was to leave. I needed to walk. I needed to smoke a cig.

Sitting on the park bench, I sparked my lighter and tried to make small talk with my sister and our friends while puffing on my cigarette. Looking around me, I saw that the trees still moved the same and the cars passed by the same as they always did. Nothing around me had changed. But I was a changed person. Six people were with me but I still felt so alone.

The thoughts racing in my head were eating away at my soul. I was empty, yet filled with emotion. Regret filled me up to my knees, the guilt filled me to my shoulders, and the rest of me was mad.

"How could he just leave us?" I asked my little sister. "He was too young to die. I was so rude to him. I didn't see him for months. There's no way he knew I loved him and if I were him I wouldn't have loved me." My sister was speechless—she just looked at me, her cheeks a light shade of pink. I stared into her hazel eyes that were glossy from crying. For a moment we were stuck in silence, just gazing at each other. She didn't know what to say to help me and I didn't know how to help myself.

Staring into the sky, watching the tree branches wave back and forth I felt the haze of remembrance cover my eyes as I thought about one of the final times I had seen my dad. The girl I once called my best friend was in town and she had arranged a kickback at Richmond Beach. I called my dad and asked him to pick up my sister and me and take us there. Dad drove us to the beach, getting lost on the way. He had grown up around this area his whole life, so I couldn't understand how it was possible for him to get lost.

As he dropped us off, he said, "Be safe and call me a half hour before you want to be picked up."

I just walked away, not saying a word. Being around him made me instantly mad. All the years of watching him choose alcohol over his kids made me despise him. He didn't even have to do or say anything; if we were in the same room I was automatically in a bad mood.

When we were ready to be picked up, we called him to let him know. He was drunk. His voice alone gave it away. His words were slightly slurred and he was making no sense, but we still needed him to pick us up. We waited in the Richmond Beach parking lot for a good half hour. I couldn't believe he would be a half hour late—that wasn't like him. When he hadn't shown up yet we called to see where he was. That's when he told us he was lost—again. Ten minutes later, he finally pulled into the parking lot and my sister and I got in the car.

"Did you guys have fun?" he asked. His eyes were so bloodshot you almost couldn't see the white. His face looked droopy and his eyes looked sunken in, the way somebody looks after they've drank too much vodka. We could tell he was drunk from the alcohol scent coming off his breath. We sat in silence the entire car ride; the only noise was the low volume of the radio. Driving along highway 99, it was clear my dad had no idea what he was doing. He kept speeding up and slowing down. When we hit a red light he would slam on the breaks so hard that we could smell the burnt rubber.

Fear paralyzed me. All I could picture was my dad losing control, leaving us to spin into another car. The twenty-minute drive home felt like an hour. He kept swerving into the lane to the right of us. My heart was beating so fast it felt like it would pound out of my chest. I was breathing so hard it sounded like I had just finished running a marathon. Each turn he made sent me sliding on the leather seats of the navy blue suburban.

"Dad, what the fuck are you doing?" I finally yelled. "This is ridiculous!" He ignored me, knowing he was in the wrong. At least in the morning he probably wouldn't remember I had cussed at him.

We finally pulled into the driveway of my little yellow house. "I love you guys. Have a good night," he said. He was upset; I could tell by the look in his eyes. He seemed disappointed in himself and as far as I was concerned, he should have been.

My sister and I ignored him and got out of the car, slamming the doors and running to the comfort and safety of our own house.

The chill of the wind blowing on my face brought me back to the park. I tried to hold back the seemingly endless tears as I walked home. My friends and sister were following in silence closely behind me. With each step I took, another memory got more and more vivid.

My dad was staying at my mom's house with my sister and me while she was in Vegas with her fiancé. We had finished our nacho dinner and I wanted to go see my boyfriend.

"Dad, we're going to Terry's house, okay?" I asked. My sister was twelve but there was no way I was going to leave her home alone with him. It was barely six o'clock and his words were already mixing together.

"Okay. Just be home in two hours," he said.

We rushed out of the house. It was dark already, so we walked the three blocks to my boyfriend's house as quickly as we could.

I got the call around 8 or 9 o'clock. "You guys need to come home now," he said. His words were so slurred I could barely understand what he was trying to say.

"Are you drunk?" I asked.

"I haven't had anything to drink," he answered in a defensive tone. "I took my pills already and I'm ready for bed. You guys need to come home." His reply was a complete lie, and he knew I knew.

I hung up the phone and turned to my sister. "Julia, Dad's drunk. Do you want to go home or what? I will do whatever you feel comfortable doing."

My sister's reply was simple. "We need to go home. I don't want to be around him if he's drunk, but we don't have anywhere else we can go." I kissed my boyfriend goodbye and we slowly walked the three blocks back to our house, both knowing the minute we got home we would be miserable.

The numb sensation in my fingers and face caused the memory to fade. But it was immediately replaced by a sudden, burning realization: I no longer had a dad. My dad was never a father figure or somebody I could look up to, but now I would never get the chance to have a good relationship with him. A jumble of awful thoughts filled my mind: I would never celebrate another Father's Day with him. He would miss my graduation, he wouldn't get the chance to walk me down the aisle, he wouldn't meet his grandkids. All I could think about were the things he wouldn't be able to do—the things we would both miss out on.

The hugs and attempted comfort meant nothing to me. The condolences, the tears—nothing could mend my pain. My dad was gone.

I turned the doorknob and walked into my house, knowing my life was forever changed.

A Note from Destiny

In the five months since my dad has passed away, I've had a lot of mixed emotions. Some days are really good and I barely think about him. On others, I can't get him out of my mind. Ironically, my dad passed away when I was finally succeeding in school, but I've used his death as motivation to become a person he would be proud of, and I've made sure not to let the loss of my dad affect my grades. A line in his favorite Trace Adkins song says, "You're gonna miss this, you're gonna want this back. You're gonna wish these days hadn't gone by so fast." I never knew song lyrics could be so relevant to my life. In the beginning I had a lot of regret about the way I treated my dad, but I have realized his love for me was, and is, unconditional. I have accepted the fact that he is gone and I have a great support system of family and close friends that help me on my bad days. I have learned to take life one day at a time, value everybody, and cherish every moment.

TAKE A BOW

KELLY PETERSON

His hair almost covers his eyes, dark black like a curtain hiding his secrets. As I drive his dad's car down the freeway, I think about the risks I'm taking: I could get a DUI. Plus, I'm risking my life. Being sixteen, there is a zero tolerance law—which means if I get pulled over and have any traces of alcohol, I'm screwed.

"It's the next exit, I think," he mumbles.

Ever since he started buying drugs more often, I have driven down here every single day. He's hooked. Drugs brought him under faster than I could keep track of. I remember when I met him in the seventh grade. He was chubby and insecure about it. Now he's skin and bones. He used to have a nice tan from being outside playing sports all day. Now he's pale; his eyes hold dark bags, as if he's been up for days. He had perfect teeth back then, too, pearly white. His favorite part about himself was by far his teeth—I swear he brushed them five times a day in the seventh grade. Now, his teeth have a tint of brown. Also, his tooth has a fake triangle right in front from fighting, causing more discoloration. Now, when I see him, I feel disappointed.

All throughout eighth grade we had the same friend group, meaning we were always together. He always tried to act like a tough guy around other people, but we became best friends because his garage was our main place to party. The garage was scum coated; the cement floors were covered in cigarette butts, spilled Four Lokos and puddles of spit. We used minivan seats as couches and a ping pong table for a beer pong. Then he started being an asshole to me and we went a whole year avoiding each other. That year was filled with just as many parties; I was just with different friends. He and I shared friends like divorced parents. I didn't hang around his house anymore and I was trying to get a fresh start at Scriber Lake High School.

But now I'm back in this pattern again because of all the mutual friends we share. Now we are more like siblings because of how often we are together and how badly we fight. Tonight is different, though. I had no intention of driving him down here when we started drinking again, almost four hours ago.

His flat-billed hat is faced down. In his lap, he holds his phone. The sounds of his keyboard clicking make me feel pressured. Every few minutes he pushes his lip over to the corner of his mouth so he can bite a certain part; his nervous habits distract me. He's texting fast enough to worry me. Since he is looking at his phone, he's paying no attention as I take the wrong exit.

I don't recognize a single thing we are driving past. Just houses. There are two lanes. Cars are parked on both sides of the road, reducing the width of the road to a single lane shared between two directions. I hate driving in this area. Seattle is a weird place to drive and this road isn't lit up well enough.

"What the fuck. Seriously? You're too drunk to drive?" he barks at me when he realizes where we are.

I feel my heart stop in rage. I try to help him and all he does is push me to hate him. He blames me for getting us lost; I blame him for giving me bad directions. Every time he wants drugs, he wants them desperately.

Ever since I was informed about his family possibly losing their house, I've tried to help him. He plans to move in with me the day the sheriff comes and physically removes him from his childhood home, but he still treats me like shit.

"I'm sorry, where do I go then?" I say. Normally I would stand up for myself. But with so much pressure, I fold. I will lose if I try that tonight. He is on a mission, and I am in his way. He doesn't answer my question, so I pull into the first place I can, a Petco parking lot. Damn, I am lost.

"Let me drive, I'm not drunk," he says. I can't tell if it's a demand or a plea. It's something about how he talks to me. I feel worthless and as if I am getting on his nerves. All I have done is safely make it to Seattle without either of us being arrested. He should be grateful.

"Whatever," I say. I doubt my decision, but I have no choice at this point. Plus, now if we get pulled over, I'm not in trouble.

I don't think I'm that drunk. I never think I'm that drunk. My day started on his couch taking straight shots of vodka within the first five minutes of waking up. Normally, we have chasers in the house, but we must have drunk it all last night. I don't remember. Days like today always end badly; I always end up what I call "white girl wasted." In that state, I can barely walk and I'll either pass out or be an evil bitch to everyone. After enough shots, I decided I needed a nap so I wouldn't end up puking or anything. Hours later, I woke up sober. It was dark by the time he had asked me for a ride.

I open the driver's side door and step out of the little white Mazda to trade places with him. Crossing paths in the front of the car, I see his glare. The headlights light up his face like he's telling a scary campfire story. I slide into the passenger side and shut the door. The automatic shoulder belt closes over my chest.

Now in the driver's seat, he continues texting until he screams, "Fuck! My phone's dying. We have to hurry!"

His yelling adds pressure to something I no longer control: how fast we get there. When I was driving, I had control. We sit there for a few seconds so he can get in contact with someone, then he gets ready to leave the Petco parking lot. He puts his phone in his lap and quickly tries to take the car out of park, except he forgets about the emergency break. I guess he didn't notice me setting it. All I can do is roll my eyes and hope I survive.

As he starts to drive I feel his speed picking up more and more. Now he's texting while driving. My anxiety builds each time he looks down at his phone.

When we finally park on a strange road, he hops out of the car, wordless, and jumps into a bright yellow jeep. He's back in five minutes, ready to drive. The look on his face shows that his drug deal went well. Now we have a new risk: drugs in the car.

I keep silent because fear has taken over my body. He doesn't say much, but he does play music from his phone.

He pulls around the corner and parks. After he turns off the car, he reaches into his pocket and pulls out a folded piece of tinfoil. I scoot as far away from him as my car seat will allow to show that I don't feel comfortable with all of this. Carefully opening it, he pulls out a tube and a lighter. The look of hate on his face has left completely; he looks happy now. Pulling out a small bag, he breaks off a piece and puts it on the foil. Lifting the foil, he burns underneath it. Smoke rises and he lets it go. He always tells me that's to get all the "cut" out, all the nasty chemicals people add to make more money. In reality, the drug itself is a nasty chemical that people use to make money. He rambles on about *anything* when he's getting high, even if it's not true. After he does that, he puts the tube in his mouth, lowers the foil and catches the smoke. After a few seconds, he exhales. The bitter scent makes me gag, but I watch his every move. I'm fascinated by how quickly his mood changes.

I don't say anything. As he puts every away, his eyes are low. He's pale, but he seems happy. When he starts the car again, he looks as if he's on top of the world. Alcohol has the same effect on me; I love it. I can't help it. When I bring up people's nasty drug use, they automatically point the finger back at me for alcohol. I know it's an issue, but so is this whole lifestyle.

The freeway entrance he chooses is extremely packed for this time of night. The risk really hits me; his driving has never made my stomach flip so often. Hanging out with my "friends" means I'm usually the one driving everywhere. Hanging out with my "friends" means that I get to sit back and watch them deteriorate, or drink myself to exhaustion with them. My opinion makes me a bitch and my thoughts make me stupid. There is no winning in the drug world—only loss. Loss of money. Loss of long-term friends. Loss of family. Loss of respect from the people who matter most, and—worst of all—loss of your own life. I wish my friends were the ones who were going to graduate high school, the ones having fun while sober, or even the ones with a little bit of hope left. I don't know how to get out of this life cycle because I can't just drop all of my closest friends at once.

I feel the speed pick up and just pray my fucked-up life doesn't turn into a final destination movie. My heart beats even faster. My right hand is clamped around the door handle. I feel my hands get clammy and I close my eyes.

I feel the first bump of the car and hear him yell, "Oh. My. God!"

"What's happening?" I scream.

My head slams into the door at my second scream because the jerk is unexpected, just like the first one. My brain doesn't know what to do with my body, so I become numb and follow the movements of the car. I'm being smacked around and I doubt the little white Mazda can take it. My shoulder strap doesn't keep me in place. Even though I'm flailing around, it doesn't hurt me a single bit. My mind is blank, as if I'm okay with dying. I knew that sooner or later my choices would kill me.

We've lost a huge amount of speed and turning the wheel is a hard task for him. The balance of the car is off, like we've lost a wheel. We barely make it out of the fast lane when I think about all the other cars on the freeway. I look over my shoulder and all I see is a sea of headlights flowing over the three lanes between safety and us.

"We have to get over!" he cries. In this sea of cars, we're shark bait. He turns the wheel once more and presses down on the gas. After more turbulence, we come to a stop on the slim shoulder.

The fact that we didn't get hit by another car on the way across three lanes is pure luck. He looks at me with his pale face and almost pukes. His "tough guy" persona has been broken. He expects me to do something. He doesn't say anything; he just gives me a *look*.

When the relief wears off, I realize half of the car is still in a car lane. Stretching inward about three feet from the cement barrier, the shoulder could provide more safety than the open lanes. The breeze of each passing car brings a gasp to my lungs; the intense speed of other cars zooming past transmits air currents, causing the car to bounce a little. The movements remind me how close we are to the passing traffic. So many things can go wrong. The cops could stop to see if we're all right and find drugs.

"Switch me spots! Holy shit. Drive the car in further. Oh my god. Help me," he says. He just now realizes that he needs me. Less than an hour ago, he was demanding to drive. Now, he's making a plea for me to take the wrath. His words hit like daggers as he stabs them into my heart, putting guilt on me. He knows that if the cops stop for us, I'll be in the driver's seat and I'll be at fault. But at least I have a license. I agree to trade places with him, like an idiot, because I know he isn't capable of getting the car all the way onto the shoulder, and it needs to be done *now*. Now I'll be even closer to cars traveling at 60 mph.

He jumps into the back as I move into the driver's seat. I hope he's set the emergency brake, even though it doesn't seem to matter at this point. I know I need to pull the strength out of me to bring us to safety. I press on the gas so hard I could send us straight into the cement barrier. But after only two uneasy bumps, we are finally safe.

Neither one of us wants to get out of the car to see the damage, so we sit in silence. I realize now that it's a tire issue and that it isn't actually his fault. I just want to blame him for putting us in the situation in the first place. Instead of getting out of the car, I call my mother.

"Mom, we broke down on the freeway," I say. "Come save us!" She's frantic, but I manage to tell her what the signs say around us so she can locate us. I avoid all other questions. I tell her to hurry, that I love her and to call his dad. His dad will be livid when he finds out what has happened to his car, so we don't want to call him.

He begins pulling foils out of every crevice of the car. He throws them out the window, over the concrete and onto the on ramp just feet away from us. He doesn't reach into his pockets for the actual drugs though. He just wants to get rid of *extra* evidence. I notice he's shaking as he lights a cigarette and I ask to hit it after him. He agrees. After that, silence strikes us like lightning.

I look over a few seconds later and notice he's getting ready to smoke again. He repeats what he did the last time we were parked, leaving him happier and less stressed. The minutes pass like hours. Every car that passes us shakes the car more and more, surprising me each time. I hope the hazard lights work as a warning signal in this devilish sea of passing headlights.

When help finally arrives, he jumps into the backseat of my mom's car and lies down, still shaking. I try to remain strong to see what happened. But anxiety takes over. I get in the back of the car with him while we wait for AAA. He rests his head on my shoulder, needing comfort. I put my arm around him and whisper, "We're alright."

We wait even more. When AAA finally comes, we give the guys his address and leave. They arrive at his house about ten minutes after us, and we finally get to see the damage. The rubber on the tire has ripped off completely, like a giant semi-truck.

At his house, I am given lots of thanks and love. The hugs keep coming from our parents. They are so thankful that we're alive that they don't think to ask why we were on the freeway at night in the first place. Knowing I didn't do much to help, I just nod and clench my fists as they rant on about me saving our lives. I feel my palms become sweaty because I'm torn between telling the truth and keeping everyone happy.

He looks up from his phone and shoots me a look of disgust. He wants all the attention, but he doesn't want me to tell what really just happened.

"I don't think I could have gotten over all three of the lanes! I'm so proud of you! Thank goodness for driver's ed!" my mom repeats over and over. By this time, we've been here for at least an hour and she's had plenty of shots.

"Yeah, it's just a tire. You can replace tires but you can't replace you guys!" his dad chimes in.

That's when it really hits me: I've been replaced. My best friend has replaced me with drugs. I suddenly begin to think about what *I've* replaced with alcohol. I'm no longer listening to the voices around me; instead, I'm trapped inside my thoughts.

I'm sick of all of this. Everyone involved in this lifestyle is only in it for their own benefit. Drugs take over a person's mind and turn them into a dirty doper. Not to mention that people on drugs aren't in their right minds and it's not fun to be around that every day. Every time I try to get out, something sucks me right back in. The money is always tempting, the people are always sketchy, and the days are always long.

※

A Note from Kelly

After only three years at Scriber, I have earned enough credits to graduate early. Most people who try to drink as often as I did have already dropped out. I still battle with recovery. Somehow, I have kept my head above water. I'm taking Running Start classes at Edmonds Community College and am planning to go there full-time next year to study early childhood education.

"Good friends are hard to find, harder to leave, and impossible to forget." —Anonymous.

I've cut the bad fruit from the tree. It took me a long time to understand that I have better chances at happiness and success on my own, away from problematic people. In this story, I expressed how I felt in the heat of that moment. I mean no harm to anyone mentioned in my story or in my past. At a certain point I had friends I called family, and although we've drifted apart, I will always love them. Even though some of it was wrong, I would never take any of it back because I learned from all the good and the bad. I still have contact with the ones I love, except I've learned to create happy and healthy relationships with some new and amazing people. Each day is a new chance to learn something; I choose to live my life that way. By writing this story I'm trying to leave behind the negatives and only carry positives into the future. The past is behind me but there's no way I could ever forget the ups and down of the last five years.

A STRIFE IN MY LIFE

CALEB "JOEY" REED

"Hey, get down from there or I am going to call the cops on you!" he says, looking up at me while blocking the sun from his eyes with his right hand.

I wish he had come when the sun was still up a bit. Then the sun would have been right behind me, burning his eyes as he looked at me. *Go ahead. Call the cops!* I think. *I couldn't care less.*

"Okay fine," I reply as I begin to come down from the roof of the Edmonds Library.

As I make my way down, trying to scheme a plan, I thoroughly scan his appearance. He wears khaki pants and a plaid shirt with a pocket protector featuring the full works. His glasses are hooked onto the inside of his shirt collar. He must work for the library.

"Hurry up, kid. I don't have all day, you know," he says with an aggravated tone.

Once on the ground, I walk over to him.

"Why were you up there, huh?" he asks.

"Because I like to be in high places," I reply.

Someone like you would never understand the real reason why I like to be on rooftops or just high places in general, I think to myself.

The reason I like high places is because I like to see the true beauty of this world. Just thinking of it right now makes me smile a bit. Above all else, I get to see the silhouettes of the mountains and the glow of the red sun in the morning lighting up the sky in a blaze of red, staining the clouds a soft magenta. There is nothing to block the view—no trees, no buildings, no people. Nothing but the sound of the wind. As you look down you see the buildings, the cars, and people like him living out their pathetic lives.

To most people, I might seem like an idiot with a death wish or something. But when I am up there, I feel like an angel or a god of some sort watching over the world from above. That is the one way that I get to feel free and powerful. When I am up in a high place, I have no regrets about anything—no worries, no pain, no anger, no sadness, no fear. I feel at peace with myself and the world. When other people get stressed out or depressed, they take some type of medication to relieve it, but that is only temporary. For me, when I am stressed out or depressed, I will find the highest place I can go, then sit back and watch the sky and clouds and listen to the wind whistling in my ears. For the first time in days or even weeks, I will finally get to actually smile and be happy. To me, it is bliss.

"What's in your backpack?" he asks.

They always ask me that. Every damn time.

"Um, papers and stuff," I answer.

"Do you have any sharpies in there?" he says, motioning again to my backpack.

"No, my mom's too poor to get me one," I say, resting my hands on the back of my head.

"So if I was to go up there and check, there won't be any graffiti on the walls up there then?" he asks, pointing his finger up to the roof.

Yeah, totally. I totally go up there where no one will be able to see anything and make a stupid gang tag that nobody will be able to read anyway. Totally.

"Uh, no. Besides, graffiti's something that all those stupid gangs do!" I state sarcastically.

"What's your name?" he asks.

"Oh, it's Caleb," I reply.

He pulls a notepad and a pen out of his chest pocket and begins to write down something on it. "Okay, Caleb. What's your last name?"

I look up at him, trying to think.

"Uh, it's Caleb Reed," I say.

He wears a nametag, but I don't get to read it fully. I don't like it that he's rushing me; things never turn out well when I am rushed by people.

"Okay, so it's Reed, spelled R-E-I-D?" he asks, holding the pen over the notepad.

"No, it's spelled R-E-E-D not R-E-I-D," I say, looking at his pen.

"Okay. Well, if I ever see you up there again, I will call the police and you will no longer be able to come onto this property again. Do you understand?"

Actually, he doesn't have to worry about that, because I never go to the same place twice. *What's the point of going to the same place over and over again when all I'll see is the same things each time?* I swear to god. They yell at me about going up there when they are the ones who have turned a blind eye to this world and the true beauties that are sitting right in front of them each and every day.

"Yes. I understand," I reply.

"Okay. You're free to go now," he says and begins to walk back to the building.

I turn away, look at the ground and let out a really big sigh, happy that this lecture is finally over. I shut my eyes and shake my head gently. I wish more people in this life were truly free.

A Note from Joey

My mind runs differently than most. When I got a brain scan it showed that the little electric currents that go on in my brain react differently when I do something compared to others. I have an IEP (Individualized Education Program), but when I took the WASL tests in elementary school, I always tested extremely high in math. I am considered a genius in that area. I've been invited into many schools for gifted children, but I could never go because my family didn't have the money for it. Ever since the fifth grade, I haven't liked the way my brain has worked, so I have tried to reprogram myself and have learned to control my emotions. At some point during my middle school years, I was suicidal. I never cut myself or tried killing myself, but I hid my true emotions behind a fake happy-go-lucky friendly front; I sealed myself. But I believe that if you dwell in the past, you'll find yourself lost in the future. So I take it one day at a time and just do what I need to do.

HERE TODAY, GONE TOMORROW

ELIZABETH TAPIA

"Ahh!" I scream as a book flies past my face. *What have I gotten myself into? Is this normal for schools in Mexico?* There is no teacher in the room and it is five minutes into class already. I don't even know what class I am in. I am basically sitting in the middle of chaos. Kids are screaming and laughing around me. Books, erasers, pencils, paper balls and other random things are being thrown.

Just a week ago I was in Seattle with my friends. Since we had to leave so quickly, I was limited to just one small suitcase. The night I found out my brother was present during a murder was when I realized that the world is a cruel place. It didn't really hit me, though, until the next day when we had to leave for Mexico to escape gang violence. I wasn't even there when it happened and I had nothing to do with it. But I still had to move to Mexico with my mom, brother and sister to what was supposed to be our vacation house. My dad had stayed behind in Seattle to work and make money for the family. I begged him to let me stay with him.

"Come on, Dad! I'll cook for you and everything! I'll get a job and I'll be good! I *promise!*" I had pleaded.

"I already told you no, Elizabeth! Stop asking me already!" he shot back.

"PLEASE!" I looked at my mom. "This isn't fair! I'm just starting to get my grades up and I'm doing so well!"

"I'm sorry, Elizabeth," my mom said.

"But why? Why can't I stay?" I asked, almost in tears.

"Because I don't even know what I'm doing or where I'm staying," my dad answered. "It would be much harder for me to find a place for the both of us than just me."

I felt the tears gathering in my eyes. I stormed out of the room, crying from sadness and anger that I would have to leave my life behind. Just like that, no goodbyes or anything.

Now I'm sitting in this middle school in Mexico as a 9th grader when I should be in 10th. They had to hold me back a grade for the language change. I have no makeup on because it's "against the rules," and I'm wearing an ugly uniform with white knee socks and ugly black shoes that are too big on my feet because they were the last ones in this tiny town with only three shoe stores. I feel like a duck. The white shirt for the uniform is also too big because the smallest size they had was two sizes too big. The brown skirt isn't as bad. The only problem is that it's too long. It stops just above my knees. But my aunt who lives in this town and went to this school is only two years older than me. She showed me how to fold it once from the top and no one will notice.

I sigh and slump down in my chair, trying to make myself invisible. But that's impossible with all these things flying around.

"Here, throw this!" says a short, chubby kid with extremely curly hair. He puts a paper ball on the corner of my desk while dodging an eraser. I sit up, look at the paper ball and grab it.

If anything like this ever happened at my school in Seattle, we would all be suspended or even expelled. I look around and see that the whole class is in on this war and no one but me is sitting at their desk. They are all yelling happily at each other and grabbing anything they can to throw across the room. *Why hasn't anyone come in and said anything about the noise?* This is the first class I've been to, and I'm wondering if this is what all my classes will be like. I roll the ball around in my hand as I think about my life in Seattle.

The last day I was there, my parents took my phone so I wouldn't be tempted to tell my best friend, Thea, where I was going or even that I was staying at my godmother's house for the night. But I did call her that night, after hours of begging my mom to use her phone. I walked out of the house into the cold air. It was October, days away from Halloween so all the houses were decorated with pumpkins. Thea and I told each other everything so she already knew that my parents said something the day before about moving to Mexico.

"Hello?" Thea's voice answered.

"Thea, listen, I don't have a lot of time," I started.

"What do you mean? I've been trying to call you all day and your phone has been off! I even tried calling your brother, mom, dad and house phone. What's going on?"

"I know and I'm so sorry I haven't been able to tell you, but..." I started to cry. "We're moving to Mexico."

"What!?" I could tell Thea was shocked. She started to cry, too. I could imagine her blue eyes filling with tears. "When? For how long?"

"Tomorrow morning. I don't know for how long. Maybe forever. We're driving to California with my cousins and we're driving across the border and then we're taking a plane from Tijuana," I said, still crying. I heard footsteps behind me and turned around to see my mom.

"Finish up your conversation. It's time to come back inside," she said. I stared at her.

"Thea, I have to go now."

"Wait!" she exclaimed.

"What?" I asked.

"What do I tell everyone when they ask me where you've been?"

"Ummm, just tell them I moved to California," I answered. She knew not to tell them more than that.

I glanced around to make sure my mom was gone.

"Oh! And…I left my window unlocked," I quickly added. "Can you go to my house tonight and grab my diary, the little cat piggy bank and my stuffed animals? My backpack is in my closet, you know. Just keep it until I come back."

I heard her sobbing louder. "Yeah, of course," she answered.

"Okay, thank you."

"I love you."

"I love you, too, Thea. Bye."

"Bye," Thea sobbed.

"Bye." I stared at the 'End' button for what seemed like forever. *This is the last conversation I'll have with her for a long time. I may never get to see my best friend again.* I finally pressed the 'end' button and I sat there for a while, wiping my tears and pulling myself together before finally going back in my godmother's house.

The bell makes me come back from my thoughts. The teacher hasn't even noticed me.

As I walk to my next class, a pretty, dark-haired girl walks up to me and says, "You know you're supposed to tell the teachers you're new here, right?"

"Oh," I answer. I didn't know, but I'm not going to tell them. I want to stay invisible as long as I can. I start walking to the back of the class.

"That's my seat," a boy says behind me, mischievously. "There's an empty seat over there, though." He smiles and points at the front of the class. I walk over and sit down without saying a word to anyone. All my classes are with the same people, but in this classroom they're all well behaved, sitting quietly and looking at the teacher. I make it through most of the class without this teacher saying anything to me, either. I'm very happy with this. But all of a sudden she taps on my desk twice. I look up and she says, "Who are you?"

"Um, my name's Elizabeth. I'm new and today's my first day," I respond.

"Did you tell your other teachers?"

"No."

"Okay, you have to tell the rest of your teachers that you're new."

"Okay, I will," I say, looking down at my desk.

I don't want to be here. I'm angry with my brother for forcing all of us to move to this small town. I'm already planning my way back to Seattle, even if I have to do it myself. I have sixty dollars from my birthday money and I plan on saving everything I get so I can leave as soon as possible.

❦

A Note from Elizabeth

People who go into gangs don't realize that it affects everyone around them. After being in Mexico for two years, I returned to Seattle with my dad and started high school at Scriber Lake. A few months later, my mom and sister came to live with us. My brother stayed in Mexico. I'm one of the oldest students at my school, but I'm proud to say that I'm getting my high school diploma. I haven't seen my brother since moving back to Seattle, but I talk to him on the phone. He's doing much better.

MAYBE I COULD HAVE SAVED HIM

NINA HOGAN

If I could just hear your voice one more time, I would tell you I love you. I would tell you that you mean the world to me and that I'm sorry.

I feel the tears running down my face. But I'm trying to stay strong and keep my cool so I wipe them away. I open the church doors and walk over to my step-mom. She is a very quiet person who doesn't really say much unless she is spoken to and never really shows her emotions.

"Where's Blake?" I ask her, biting my lip to keep my voice from trembling.

"Three doors down on the left," she says with a blank stare.

I walk down the hallway clenching a note in one hand while wiping smeared makeup off my face with the other. I get to the third door, stop and take a deep breath. Then I slowly walk in. I see numerous people surrounding a coffin, with a plaque next to it reading "R.I.P. Blake." I make my way through the crowd and get to the open casket. My palms are sweating and I start to feel sick. I don't want to look. But I can't help but stare.

I hold the note so tightly in my hand that it is wrinkled and damp from my sweat. I place it in the open casket, trying to hold back anger and sadness. Even though I know I'm not alone, I feel like a piece of me is missing. He and I were never really close, so I only called him Blake. I had been waiting for the right time to tell him I loved him and to call him "Dad."

My thoughts are beating against my head, punishing me for my mistake. *When I want to say something to someone, I need to just say it from now on,"* I chastise myself. *I can't hold back what I have to say because I never know when someone is just going to be gone out of my life. Forever.*

The people surrounding the casket look at me. I hear a lady whisper to her friend, "We should give his daughter some time alone with him."

I pull up a chair next to Blake and just sit there, looking down at him and twiddling my thumbs, not knowing what to think. Should I say something to him? He looks so pale and when I touch him, he feels so cold. There is a faint smell of old people in the room, which is weird because I don't consider him old. He was only fifty-one. Then I remember that I'm in an old rundown church. *It's just the church smell, not Blake.* I'm talking in my head like a third person.

He's wearing his big round glasses and I notice that his bald head is shining. He is dressed in a nice suit, with his hands crossed; it looks like he is sleeping. *I wish he would just wake up already.* I know that he can't hear me, but I've been pretending like he can since the day he passed away.

As I sit and think about what to say, I remember the last time I saw him. It was two summers ago and I was in the 5th grade. My mom and I had gone to visit Blake in Brewster, Washington, for the Omak stampede, a huge festival with carnival rides and a rodeo. We ended up staying out until late that night, going on every single ride and eating carnival food until we couldn't eat any more. It was one of the best nights of my life. I felt like I had a family, finally.

We didn't make the trip this past summer because my mom and I didn't have enough money to drive to Brewster. Now, just months later, Blake is lying in a casket before me. I can't shake the regret I feel. *I should have just visited him. My mom had enough money, I know she did. I should have kept in better contact with him. Maybe I could have saved him.*

My mom had told me about Blake's death just after I had returned from a fun day with my best friend, Madi. I was in a great mood when

I walked through the front door and dropped my heavy purse onto the floor. But it changed when I saw my mom. She greeted me with a look that made me think she was holding back anger—like she was mad about something.

"Nina, I need you to come upstairs with me," she said in a flat, serious tone as she picked up my purse.

I climbed the stairs, thinking of every possible thing that could have gone wrong. *Nina it's probably not that bad, so stop worrying.*

We got to my mom's room and I stood by the end of her bed. She closed the door behind me. When she turned to look at me, I saw that her eyes were puffed up.

"You should sit down for this," she said.

"No, mom you're scaring me. Come on, Who died? Ha-ha," I laughed, thinking I was being funny.

I knew by the look she shot me that something horrible had happened. My heart started pumping and all I could think of was the worst. She pulled out a stuffed animal that looked like a sheep, a necklace with a cross on it and a book with the title "Heaven for Kids."

"Here, I want you to have these," she said softly.

"What is this for?" I asked, confused.

"Nina, Blake had a heart attack last night and didn't make it."

My vision went blurry, my knees buckled and my body collapsed on the floor. I felt weak, like someone had just taken my heart and stomped on it.

"No!" I screamed.

My mom, trying to help, pulled me up and held me in her arms while I cried like I had never cried in my life. My life suddenly just didn't make sense. *Why him? Why did HE have to die?* I wanted to throw up, but the clenched feeling in my stomach made it so I couldn't even breathe.

I never thought I could ever feel such pain—that anyone could ever feel that much pain.

I pulled away from my mom, walked into my bathroom, took a deep breath and looked at myself in the mirror. *Who is going to walk me down the aisle? What about Father's Day? What about graduation?* I wiped away the pain falling from my eyes.

I'm still sitting next to Blake's open casket, staring down at him, when my mom comes into the room.

"It's time to get seated, Nina. The memorial is about to start," she says softly.

I stand up from my chair and take one last look at Blake. I know what I have to do.

I lean toward the casket and grab the note I had written to him. Still damp, I unwrinkle it and whisper the words I had written the day before.

"I love you, Daddy. Rest in paradise."

I feel my mom hugging me. "Everything will be okay, baby girl."

As my mom and I walk out to the memorial and sit down, the music starts to play. My mind is blank. *Breathe, Nina, you're stronger than you seem.*

A Note from Nina

I am now eighteen years old and have grown up a lot. I now know not to dwell on the little things people say, especially when they're close to you. I make sure to end the day on a good note, even if I've had a fight with someone that day. I am in my senior year of high school, just about to graduate, and plan to enroll in community college next year. I am proud to say that I am very happy with the way my life is going now. I have learned to overcome things because of the struggles that I have experienced and now I actually think before I act. You only get stronger with the experiences that life throws at you, so when you don't think you can handle a situation, think again. You're stronger than you seem.

MY JOURNEY TO ALICE

CORINNA J. FLAHERTY

I am standing in a boiling bathroom in a town I do not know, in a state where I do not belong.

I stare, dumbfounded, at the two tiny pink lines on the stupid lying plastic stick. No words come to mind; I am frozen, unable to think, speak or even move as warm, wet streaks fall down my face in a rush of liquid. I look up from the stick to the reflection of my puffy, burning maroon cheeks in the mirror. *This is a lie. The mirror is an illusion. That is not my face.*

I slowly slide to the tile floor and lay my face on its comforting solidness. I close my eyes and try to block out the world around me and just focus on the cool green tile squares under my sinking body. The little ridges where one tile meets the other dent my face. I feel like I am melting into the stability of the floor beneath me. Suddenly I feel wetness and acknowledge the furry, loving, slobbering face that is unaffected by my despair.

"Oh Digby. What am I going to do?" I whimper with fear to the fuzzy Jack Russell Terrier.

He continues to look at me with those loving, chocolate brown eyes and gives me an encouraging nudge with his cold, wet nose. He thinks it is high time that the king of the house had some attention. So I pull myself up and walk the long, narrow road to the park. I play fetch with the little prince and note how vibrantly green the leaves are. Even the little strands of grass are lit up with color and life. Children are playing baseball on the field, their cheeks flushed with color from the sun. For a moment, I feel peaceful.

Then my phone rings. It's Josh. I take a deep breath, trying to slow my heart attack-worthy heartbeat, and answer the phone.

"Hello?" I say in a calm voice, trying to hide my true feelings.

But I know he can hear the shakiness of my nerves even through the phone because he immediately asks, "What's wrong?"

His velvety voice reverberates in my tingling red-hot left ear and makes me unable to answer his simple question. All at once it's like a bomb hits and I start to bawl my eyes out. I do not fit here in this park scene with the sounds of children laughing, dogs barking and parents conversing around me. I want so badly to be back on that stable, safe bathroom floor.

"Hello?" His voice is urgent and worried. "Corinna? Are you there? What happened?"

He is starting to sound frantic. But all I can do in response is cry harder. I cry so hard the ground seems to shake beneath me.

"If you don't tell me what happened I can't help you. Please let me help you."

I can picture his face creased with worry, his brown eyes clouded with fear.

"I'm pregnant," I practically whisper into the now-drenched phone. Even though I whisper it, I swear the parents of all the children around me hear me. They look at me with pity and disgust. It's silent on the other end for a lifetime, but finally he says, "Oh." That's it. All he has to say is "oh." My heart drops as I think to myself *He is going to tell me how stupid I am and that he never wants to talk to me again.*

After another lifetime pause he says the most magical words in the world. "Well, you need to come home, then. I need to be with you." He says this with an air of finality.

"How? How is that supposed to work?" I practically scream at him, daring him to challenge me and tell me those magic words again.

"Then I will come to you. We will figure this out. You are not alone."

His words send a sense of grounding back into my body, but I reply, "I can't ask you to do that for me. We would have nowhere to live. What would we do?"

I am in awe that he has even suggested this because he has never left Edmonds, Washington, before and he's suddenly willing to travel three thousand miles across the country to be with me in Massachusetts. I feel so much love for him in this moment it is unreal. Just four months ago we were both so depressed living in his parents' basement that I hated his guts.

I start the walk back to the house where I am staying with the man I had used as an escape. If I had felt I had another option to escape my desire to die, I would have never come to Massachusetts. What was supposed to be a vacation from how alone I felt had turned into something a little more permanent. The whole point was to get away from my depression. But my problems had followed me, and they were just getting worse.

I'd been living in Massachusetts for two months when my grandfather died and I had to return to Washington for a week for his funeral. While there, I ended up seeing Josh again. We reconnected and I fell in love with him all over. It caused a lot of mixed emotions and confusion. *What should I do? Where should I be?* But I had made the wrong choice and returned to Massachusetts. Now I know I should have just stayed home with Josh.

When I get back to the house, the man I hate is waiting for me, holding the evil stick of lies in his left hand.

Great. This day is about to get even worse. I sigh as he looks down at me and says, "What the fuck is this?"

My heart trembles as I wait for what is to come. I am unable to answer him or even keep eye contact. Digby jumps up to tell me he wants a treat. I try to squeeze past him through the narrow hallway to get to the kitchen.

"I said...what the fuck is this?" he barks at me as he blocks my path.

I flinch from our close contact and look up at him with fear. "It's a pregnancy test, obviously," I say, dripping with sarcasm.

"Don't be a smart ass, you little bitch. When were you planning on telling me we are having a child?" His disdain seeps into my skin.

WE aren't having anything, I think to myself. "Well, I just found out about an hour ago so I was going to let myself process it before I tried to involve anyone else," I tell him. I choose my words carefully so he will just let me pass.

"Well this is just fucking perfect timing," he spits as he shoves past me and storms out the front door to return to work. When I hear the sound of his car start and drive away I release what feels like a brick of oxygen from my lungs. I make my way through the now peaceful hallway, getting to the kitchen in enough time to give the little prince his treats before he has a panic attack from lack of delicious puppy crack.

It's nearly midnight and I'm pretending to be asleep when I hear the front door open and his heavy footsteps climb the stairs, getting closer to my hiding spot under the covers. My heart skips as I hear the bedroom door open. I squeeze my eyes shut as if that alone will block out the fear that has consumed my whole body, freezing it into a piece of glass ready to shatter at the slightest touch. About an hour before, he had stormed out after throwing a laptop at my head, leaving me curled in a ball, bawling on the couch.

He turns on the light and says, "I know you're not sleeping; I don't know why you even try to pretend." All I can do is squeeze my eyes shut while clenching my body, trying to stay still. He throws the blanket off me and pulls me up by my wrists.

I say the only thing I can think of that will save my life. "I'm getting an abortion."

He stops and stares at me with shock. Then, like a wave, I see the rage fill his eyes. He shoves me down on the bed with such force that my neck bounces. I kick him in the chin, but he grabs the pillow and uses it to smother my face. He puts his entire body weight on it, causing my teeth to penetrate my bottom lip. I taste blood; I can't breathe. I'm suffocating. *I'm dying.* I stop struggling.

"You stupid whore! You will not murder my child!" He is yelling but everything is muffled. "You will not murder my child. You will not murder my child," he says, over and over again.

The more he repeats it, the angrier I get. My body is suddenly filled with such rage that I have the power to push him away and make a run for the door, sucking in all the air I can. I get to the doorway and have my hand on the cold doorknob when he pulls me back. I find myself on my back, staring up at the man who has caused me to choke on the blood pooling in the back of my throat. I hear a voice in my head say, *Go home Corinna. It's not safe here anymore.*

Somehow I find the strength to pull myself up and dart frantically down the stairs and out the door into the security of the cool, spring-night air. I run away from him and his words, vowing never to turn back. I run for what seems a year but is only a mile and a half. He chases me in his car. I run up and down back streets, darting to and from poky bushes, getting needles stuck in my hair. I stop and sit behind a cluster of bushes in some rich person's front lawn. I know he is close because I can hear his stereo blaring Rihanna and Chris Brown's "Birthday Cake" as he drives up and down the street. As I hide in the bush, I move a branch and can see the rage morphing his face through his car window. Suddenly, he sees me. His expression changes to blood thirst.

I don't know where else to go. I look around and see a field. I stand up and run. I run across the empty street and onto the empty field. Thinking I'm safe, I let my mind wander to my feet squishing in the mud. But to my surprise he drives onto the field after me. My heart has accelerated so fast I feel my body tremble with every pump of blood through my veins. I can no longer enjoy the comfort of the mud—now it's trying to hold me back. I dart to the side, through some bushes and run up a familiar street that seems to go on forever until I get to my friend's apartment. I break into his bedroom window and slide right into his bottom floor apartment. He helps me clean my face so I don't look like a zombie, gives me words of comfort and a kitty to pet as I sit on his bed, sobbing. He hides me until the morning. I go to school with him the next day, just to feel safe. We practically run to his car in case I'm still being followed.

I call Josh on the ride. "I want to come home," I cry to him.

"What happened?" he asks, startled by my tone.

"Nothing. I just want to come home, now," I plead.

"Okay. I'll buy the plane ticket." He is speaking the words of angels.

"That's perfect, thank you," I say.

After school my friend drops me back at his apartment and then returns with some clothes and necessities. The next day he drives me to the airport. I get on the plane with almost nothing; everything else is left in that house of horrors.

Seven Months Later

I look around the ice-cold room and see a metal sink against the far wall. A warm red coats the walls of the tiny office. A mass of machines and monitors are hooked up, like large jewels hanging off an elegant silver string.

"Would you like to know the sex?" the ultrasound technician asks.

I look up and nod, "Yes."

"It's a girl."

I smile with tears in my eyes and say, "I'm going to name her Alice."

A Note from Corinna

My best friend saved my life that day. It's been about a year since the incident I described in this story and now I get to look into the eyes of the most precious baby girl in the whole world. My life has become more stable and I am able to make wiser decisions for myself and my daughter. Life has really turned around and shown me that everything that happens is a lesson. The lesson I learned from this story is to follow my gut and I will never be wrong. I am in the process of moving into my own apartment and am actively looking for work. Alice and I currently live with Josh and we are learning to be a happy, yet still dysfunctional, family. Things are starting to look up, and even though my biggest fears came true, I dealt with every situation and am now filled with hope for my future. I welcome this new feeling of hope. I am now working on getting my diploma. One thing I know for sure is that Alice will go to Europe (with me) and to college.

FRI(END)S

LUPITA RUELAS

Take a hit—it will make you feel good, a voice in my head says. *Remember why you cried last night and the night before? All that pain will be gone in seconds... just take a hit.*

Like every other morning on my way to school, I catch the #116 bus to the beach in downtown Edmonds. I'm sitting in the back of the bus where I can smell the cigarettes of the person sitting next to me. I have my earphones in place listening to "Lonely Star" by The Weekend because I can't stand all the commotion and noise of the bus. As soon as the bus comes to a complete stop I look outside my window and see my "friend" Kristina. She is sitting outside on a bench, a pipe in her mouth, trying not to make it obvious that she is smoking a bowl when in reality that's exactly what she's doing. I see my other "friend" Melanie walk off the bus to join Kristina. *Are you fucking kidding me? Can you be any more stupid?* I say to myself.

I get up and walk to the bus driver. "Hey, is it okay if I stay on?" I ask. "It's too cold to wait outside."

It is not really too cold to wait outside. But I know that if I step off that bus, I won't be able to resist smoking; I could really use it at the moment.

"Sure, and thank you for asking," the bus driver replies.

The second bus I catch to school won't leave for another seventeen minutes. I walk back to my seat, ready to put my earphones in, when I see Melanie and Kristina walk into some bushes by the beach. *Wow, they don't even invite me. Whatever. I see how it is, I don't need them.* The truth is that deep down I'm jealous it's not me with the pipe in my mouth.

Melanie and I have known each other for seven years. We clicked instantly and at one point, we were inseparable. We have the same taste in everything, and she's short just like me. People have even told us we look alike and that we were like butt cheeks, because wherever one went the other went. But it's not like that anymore. I met Kristina five years ago when I moved to the Lynnwood/Edmonds area from North Seattle. I couldn't stand one bit of her; she was just so annoying. At one point I wanted to beat the living crap out of her and I couldn't think of a reason why.

I moved to Washington from California when I was ten. My parents wanted to give me a better lifestyle away from the violence and drugs, when really they messed up my life even more.

My dad felt that I had changed when we got here. His words replayed over and over in my head. "What happened to you? To the sweet little girl I used to know? What happened to my daughter?" I could see the hurt in his eyes.

"I grew up, Dad," I had replied when he said this, no emotion in my voice.

He didn't realize how it had affected me when he and my mom took me away from my relatives and my childhood friends. *Is it selfish to say that my parents are the main reason I want to pull the plug on my life at times?*

The only place I feel safe is in my room, knowing that once I step out, it's a world full of constant arguing and verbal abuse. The night before I had walked into the kitchen from my room with an empty bowl in my hands. I accidently bumped into my brother and dropped the bowl. Broken glass shattered everywhere. "Shit!!" I muttered under my breath.

My dad had turned to look at me from the other side of the kitchen. "Are you retarded?" he yelled. "What the fuck is your problem? Are you stupid or something? Damn! Can't you do anything right? You're useless."

I flinched at the sound of his angry voice and shot him the nastiest look ever. Without saying a word, I picked up the broken glass and walked back to my room.

Usually, on other nights, I would get in my dad's face and we would yell at each other for hours. Then I would lock myself in my room and cry, wait for everyone to fall asleep, open my window and take out the dub of weed I hid in a sock under my mattress. I would smoke it until all the pain was gone.

I sat on my bed and cried. I felt so alone, so hopeless. *I'm useless, retarded, I can't do anything right. No one cares about me. Why can't I just be perfect? Why do I even exist?* I wanted to cut myself until the last and final drop of blood was gone from my body. I snapped out of it and lay on my cold bed crying.

Forgive me, God. I am a sinner and I shall sin again. I sobbed until I passed out from exhaustion.

The phone call from Melanie snaps me back to the bus.

"Hey, do you want to come smoke?" she asks. I can hear Kristina laughing in the background.

I think about last summer. I had spent an entire week in Eastern Washington at La Cima, a bilingual leadership camp. I remember the words of my mentor, Barbie. "You can be anything you want to be. It's a matter of how bad you want it," she had told me. I had always settled for less because I thought I wasn't smart enough or didn't have the potential to be someone in life, so her words had affected me significantly.

The reason I had gone to the camp was to get my life back together. While there, I heard the story of Vincent Perez, the founder of La Cima.

His life was a struggle. He had run away from his abusive dad with his mom and brothers. He told us how had to build his way up to the top, starting from nothing. But he did it, which now motivates me to keep going. The last day I was at camp, I was encouraged to write a letter to myself and mail it to myself. I had just received it a couple of weeks earlier. I remembered the words I wrote:

"Now I know that there are people that care that will be here for you. You don't need 'worthless' things in your life to make me feel better because there are real people living similar and worse situations. So every time you feel down, remember that there are people that care and never give up. Always make something positive out of every negative situation. XOXO- Lupita."

I think about the letter before I respond to Melanie's invitation to smoke. *I could use it, but is it really worth getting high just to balance out my lows?*

"Um, no thanks. I'll pass," I respond. A couple of minutes later, Kristina and Melanie walk on the bus. They have the giggles. *Ugh.* I roll my eyes. They sit behind me; I don't think I have ever been more annoyed in my life. I have my earphones in place, but I am not listening to music; I am eavesdropping on their conversation.

"Are you coming or not?" Kristina says, sounding like she is losing patience.

"No, I don't want to be late," Melanie responds.

"We're not going to be late! Come on," Kristina urges.

"No, after school, I promise," Melanie says, and gives her a sweet smile.

Kristina wants Melanie to go off and smoke with her one last time before school starts. "Talk about peer pressure," I say under my breath.

One bus stop before we get to school, I see Kristina get off. I arrive to school and walk into the lunchroom with Melanie following behind me. I don't expect her to sit next to me because we haven't been talking lately;

I figure she does it because Kristina isn't there.

"How you been?" she asks and then cuts me off before even letting me respond. "Why don't you talk to us anymore?" She sounds upset.

"I don't know," I say, looking down at the table.

I don't feel like talking about it at the moment. I know if I get into the subject I am going to lose patience really fast, and I'm really not in the mood for arguing, especially not with Melanie. In our whole seven years of being friends, we have never fought.

"You think you're too cool for us now?"

I let out a little laugh and look up at her, "To cool for you? Ha! If I was to cool for you guys I would talk to other people. Do you see me talking to other people? No you don't!"

I am really annoyed.

"Then what is it?" she asks in a calm voice.

"Every time I am around, you guys never talk to me. You always exclude me out of everything or you are always doing things I'm not up to. I'm not about to be your little side hoe, following you around when I can feel the tension and know I'm not wanted," I respond.

My words are only partially true. The real truth is that I just want to change and be a better person and have friends who support me with my new goals. It seems pointless to get advice from someone who is high or who is going to bring me down. All they seem to care about is smoking and I don't need that in my life anymore. I just wish she could see how hurt I am.

"But we're friends, or does our friendship not matter to you anymore?" I feel a cold shiver down my spine when she says that.

"I don't know. It's whatever, really," I respond.

"Wow are you—?" The first bell rings and it cuts her off. I get up and leave the room.

A Note from Lupita

I am now seventeen years old, a junior at Scriber Lake High School, and school is my first priority. I will be graduating next year and college is definitely in my plans. I hope to become a juvenile probation officer. My goal is to help young adults stay out of trouble before it is too late. I have a boyfriend I've been dating for the past eleven months. He has helped me to become the better person I am today. He reminds me every day that I am not alone. I have been sober for eight months and I am taking the relationship with my parents one step at a time. I have learned to embrace myself and not to try to be someone I am not. I have learned that people enter and exit your life, and that sometimes exits are for the best.

HOW WE STARTED

INGRID RICKS

Marjie Bowker and I had no idea we were launching a teen publishing program when we first decided to partner in January of 2012. Our only goal was to a teach month-long narrative nonfiction-writing course using my coming-of-age memoir, *Hippie Boy: A Girls' Story.*

Marjie, who is always looking for innovative ways to make her English classes relevant and empowering for her students, felt *Hippie Boy* was a perfect fit for her students because it deals with a teen overcoming obstacles and carries a message of hope and empowerment that she wanted them to hear. We started brainstorming and soon Marjie was crafting a curriculum that used *Hippie Boy* as a guide to help her students claim their power by writing their personal stories in a narrative format.

Our month-long partnership was supposed to end with an in-class reading of the students' work. But by the time the reading rolled around, the students were so charged up by the power they had found within themselves that Marjie and I realized we had to keep going. With the full support of Scriber Lake Principal Kathy Clift, we decided to offer an intensive weeklong mini-course to help interested students turn their draft life scenes into finished stories and publish them in a group story collection. A month later, our first teen story collection, *We Are Absolutely Not Okay: Fourteen Stories by Teenagers Who Are Picking Up the Pieces,* debuted as an eBook on Amazon. Two weeks later, the paperback was available for purchase.

By writing and publishing their stories, the student authors involved have overcome painful situations from their pasts and are taking charge of their lives. They are also connecting with other struggling teens—

letting them know that life does get better.

Having experienced the enormous validation and empowerment that comes from personal storytelling, Marjie and I are committed to continuing our teen mentoring/publishing program to help Scriber Lake students—and teens everywhere—claim their power by writing and sharing their stories.

WHO WE ARE

Scriber Lake is an alternative high school in the Edmonds School District, located just north of Seattle, Washington. Ours is a school of choice; some students come to Scriber as freshmen, some come seeking a second chance, and some land here for a last chance. The majority of Scriber students have felt lost in the system at some point and many find success in our program. We are a school of small classes and caring teachers who strive toward creative approaches to learning. Scriber is a family.

Though this program is being spearheaded at Scriber Lake, we view the We Are Absolutely Not Okay mentoring/publishing program as the beginning of a grassroots movement that helps teens everywhere claim their power by finding their voice and sharing their stories.

For more information, please visit www.weareabsolutelynotokay.org.

PROGRAM MENTOR

Marjie Bowker has taught English and a little history somewhere in the world for the past 16 years: in China, Norway and Vietnam, in addition to her "regular" spot at Scriber Lake High School in the Edmonds School District just north of Seattle, Washington. A strong advocate of community/ student partnerships, she is constantly fostering relationships with community leaders to help enrich the lives of the teens she works with and was recently recognized as "Teacher of the Year" by the local VFW chapter for her innovative teaching/mentorship style. Past awards include two NEH scholarships to study at Columbia University and Crow Canyon Archaeology Center. Marjie has traveled to more than thirty countries and is always on the lookout for creative ways to infuse her love of travel into her teaching career, including leading two trips to Costa Rica to save the Leatherback sea turtles.

PROGRAM MENTOR

Ingrid Ricks is a Seattle-based journalist, author, marketing consultant and mentor who is passionate about leveraging the new world of digital publishing and print-on-demand to give teens a voice. Ingrid's essays and stories have been published in *Salon, Ladies' Home Journal, The Advocate* and a variety of other publications. She has also shared her stories on the national NPR show, *Snap Judgment* and KUOW Presents, a Seattle NPR affiliate. Ingrid is the author of three books: *Hippie Boy: A Girl's Story,* a coming-of-age memoir; *Focus,* a memoir about her journey with the blinding eye disease Retinitis Pigmentosa; and *A Little Book of Mormon (and Not So Mormon) Stories,* a short story collection. She is currently working on *Determined to See,* a memoir about her yearlong quest to heal her eyesight. For more information, visit www.ingridricks.com

ACKNOWLEDGMENTS

This teen mentoring/publishing program would not be possible without the ongoing encouragement and support of Scriber Lake Principal Kathy Clift. From the beginning, she has understood the power of these voices and the importance of ensuring that they are heard.

We are grateful to the Hazel Miller Foundation for awarding us a grant that ensures the continuation of our program through the 2013/2014 school year. We are also grateful to the Rotary Club of Edmonds Daybreakers, who have been avid supporters of both our teen mentoring/publishing program and Scriber Lake High School as a whole.

Finally, we want to extend a special thank you to the Edmonds Bookshop for supporting our books and teen authors; to IndieReader. com for spotlighting *We Are Absolutely Not Okay* on their website throughout the year, and to Risa Laib, a gifted editor who volunteered her time to proofread this manuscript.